D0051482

God Is *Able*

God Is *Able*

Priscilla Shirer

Nashville, Tennessee

Copyright © 2013 by Priscilla Shirer
All Rights Reserved
Printed in the United States of America

978-1-4336-8191-2

Published by B&H Publishing Group
Nashville, Tennessee

Dewey Decimal Classification: 248.843
Subject Heading: GOD \ ANXIETY \ WOMEN

Unless otherwise stated, Scripture is taken from the
New American Standard Bible (NASB), © the Lockman
Foundation, 1960, 1962, 1963, 1968, 1971, 1972, 1973,
1975, 1977; used by permission.

Also used: The Holy Bible, New International Version (NIV),
copyright © 1973, 1978, 1984, 2011 by International Bible
Society.

Also used: The New Living Translation (NLT), copyright 1996,
2004. Used by permission of Tyndale House Publishers, Inc.,
Wheaton, Illinois 60189. All rights reserved.

Also used: *The Message*, the New Testament in Contemporary
English, © 1993 by Eugene H. Peterson, published by NavPress,
Colorado Springs, Colorado.

Also used: English Standard Version® (ESV®), copyright © 2001
by Crossway, a publishing ministry of Good News Publishers.
Used by permission. All rights reserved."

Also used: Holman Christian Standard Bible (HCSB), Copyright
© 1999, 2000, 2002, 2003, 2009 by Holman Bible Publishers.
Used by permission.

1 2 3 4 5 6 7 • 17 16 15 14 13

DEDICATION

I was only a teenager when a young preacher stood behind the pulpit in my church and taught a message on Ephesians 3:20–21. I was riveted. Every word was like a match striking a fire in the depths of my soul—a fire that has never dwindled in the two decades since.

This book is dedicated to that preacher.

Richard Allen Farmer, thank you for being a faithful student of God's Word, declarer of God's truth, and servant to the body of Christ. You are a trustworthy friend and loving pastor to Jerry and me, and . . . we are grateful.

CONTENTS

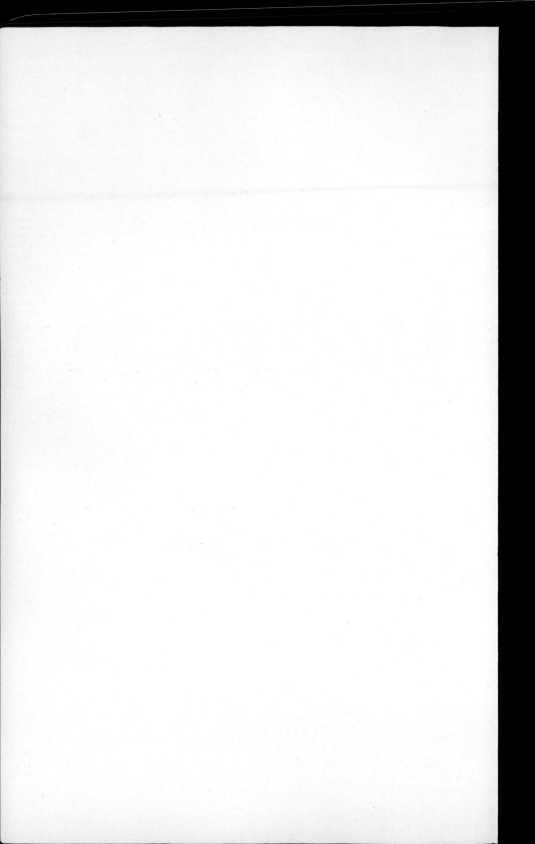

Tell Me

What is it?

Come on, you can tell me.

I know there's something specific that brought you to this book or brought this book to you.

Because everybody's got *something*.

No matter who you are, however old or young, there's always at least one thing. That thing in your life you can't seem to—you know, escape or fix or solve. It's just . . . it's . . .

(Sigh.)

It's always there. Just when you think you've maybe figured out a little piece of it—how you might be able to handle it better, manage it, work around it, or get out ahead of it—it always seems to end up beating you, or at least keeping you awake in the wee hours of the night.

You've tried. (Oh, Lord, how you've tried.) You've prayed. You've asked. You've begged. You've fretted. You've calculated. You've eaten better. You've exercised more.

You've tried being gentler, then firmer. Louder, then quieter. More assertive, then more submissive. You've admitted where you went wrong and refused to gloat when you were right. You feel like you've done everything you can think of. And honestly, you're starting to seriously wonder now if God can do this, if He can do . . . *It*.

You'd still like to think He can. And if you were to spout all your churchy rhetoric, it'd sure sound like you believe He can. But deep down—down where your soul pulses with doubt and uneasiness—you wonder about that circumstance, that life issue, that dilemma you're facing. God may be able to keep the stars in the sky, the earth tilted on its axis, and the heavens hung in glorious array. But can He do *this*?

It?

What is it? It's okay. Be honest. Name it.

Might make it easier on you, I guess, if I go first, huh? So I'll start . . . 'cause, you know, I've got a few *Its* myself.

Surprised? You shouldn't be.

Here, hold my purse while I climb down from whatever pedestal you may have placed me on so we can talk eye to eye.

I know how it happens: you see a speaker on stage, you listen to a teacher on the radio, you read the words of an author, and somehow you think they've got it all together.

I've done the same thing. Catapulted that mere human to superhuman status, as if someone so obviously godly couldn't possibly struggle with the same problems the rest of us face. They're just a little too special for life to treat them that way.

But I've found it's just not true. Nobody is exempt from these things. Like you, I've seen my share of situations that have been so difficult or have caught me so off guard, they've carved out a deep foothold where doubt could settle in. And yet God loves me far too much—same as He loves you—to keep me from confronting them. Because if you and I didn't turn to face these things, we'd never come face to face with Him. And our God's not having any of that.

So, yes, I'll start:

- Fifteen years ago, I didn't believe He could heal my broken heart.
- Twelve years ago, I wasn't certain He'd be able to save my marriage.
- Ten years ago, I wondered if He was able to let me safely bear a child.
- Eight years ago, I questioned if He could ease a heavy cloak of guilt and regret I was harboring.
- Five years ago, I had only a thin shred of hope that He could salvage a cherished friendship.

✤ Four years ago, I didn't see any way we could purchase a key piece of property we needed.

✤ Three years ago, I had little faith He could heal my son of some troubling emotional issues.

✤ Two years ago, I doubted He could free me from a paralyzing sense of fear and anxiety.

✤ And even as recently as last year, I seriously questioned if I was suited for the ministry God had entrusted to me. In fact, I questioned it enough that in my darkest moments, I considered throwing in the towel.

And listen, that's just the past fifteen years. I'll spare you my whole life story in hopes you won't check me off your reading list.

(All right, I'm finished now. You can hand me back my purse.)

The fact is, I have never had much trouble believing in the power of God when it was theoretical, when all the action my faith required of me was saying "Amen" during a sermon. As long as the problem was somebody else's, I could believe in God's big-time ability with a big old sense of gusto.

Like when I was a kid, for instance. I remember "testimony service" at my childhood church like it was yesterday. A couple of Sunday evenings a month, folks would come forward to declare the work of God in their lives. No doubt one of the ladies would be sporting her coordinating suit and fancy church hat (with a feather or some other décor hanging off of it) as she stood in front of the congregation and filled the microphone with all the things God had been up to. Everything from the foreclosure notice on her house, the repossession order for her car, her unfaithful husband, or her rebellious child being miraculously transformed by God's miracle-working power. As children, my siblings and I would sit in the pews during this stirring part of the service, listening to the lady's voice grow deeper and more forceful with each new revelation. That feather on top of her velvet hat would dance a little jig, which would always capture our attention. We tried to listen—promise we did—but sometimes we couldn't help but nudge each other and giggle. We were hoping beyond hope that her hat—or at least the bouncy feather on it—would come flying off her head into the front pew, just to make things really exciting. But Mommy wasn't having any of that. She'd tell us to quiet down and sit up straight—and listen. So we did. Then we applauded with the rest of the congregation in celebration of what God could do . . . and was actually doing.

Yup, faith seemed easier then.

But not anymore. When I'm staring now at my *own* dilemmas, trying to keep the hat of sanity on my *own* head, a little seed of doubt surprises me by taking root and often blossoming into a whole forest of questions about His ability and/or willingness to take care of them.

Somehow, I think you can relate.

In the midst of these various challenges and struggles that come together to threaten my sense of security, stability, and balance, I've found my worst fears confirmed. I am insufficient, outmatched, and incapable of fixing everything. Sometimes I don't know how I'm going to make it through the day. But I've also learned something else—something that has changed my entire life.

God is able.

Time and again, He has proven very plainly to me that He is not held down by what holds us. He has bowled me over with His capacity and inclination to do the unthinkable, both in my own life as well as in the lives of others. As surely as He's tested me, He has also given me testimony. And it would be a grand cover-up on my part not to tell His part of the story in the same big, bold colors.

For instance . . .

· · · · · · · · · · · · · · · ·

A nine-year-old boy in my church was diagnosed with a brain tumor that stunned us all.

Nine years old.

Doctors said if the cancer didn't claim his life, the required surgeries would almost certainly claim his memory and severely alter his personality. So against this kind of desperate, disheartening backdrop, we stopped what we were doing and we prayed. And God heard (as He always does) and answered—clearly, miraculously, powerfully.

Saw this young man at a gathering just last month. He's sixteen now, and I can tell you he's a lot more worried about what the girls think of him now than what the doctors do.

He's healed. He's whole.

It's done.

. . . .

After twenty-five years, my friend's husband decided to leave her. Ran off to a lifestyle that seemed more appealing to him than the monotonous, daily rhythm of matrimony. So she prayed. *For five solid years!* And wouldn't let herself doubt that God could answer (seeing as how other Christians seemed to be doing enough doubting for her).

But God set us straight one bright Sunday morning when our pastor called that husband forward in the middle of service and stood him by the altar. Couldn't believe it. None of us had seen him in years. But there he was, all dressed up in a suit and tie.

Then the back doors of the sanctuary swung open, the pianist let out a stirring rendition of "Here Comes the Bride," and here she came—the bride—the same bride who had walked the aisle to greet this same man thirty years earlier. Their children and grandchildren played the roles of bridesmaids and groomsmen, standing around them while the restored couple stood hand in hand at the altar. And when they said "I do". . .

It was done.

Most memorable Sunday morning of our lives.

. . . .

Not too long ago, I was struggling so desperately with fear and insecurity, I thought I had lost my mind and was about to lose my ministry. Opportunities to speak and share were abounding, but for some reason I felt utterly paralyzed, immobilized, demoralized by a cloaking sense of dread and anxiety that held on to me more tightly than a toddler to the hemline of his mama's skirt.

That's not a good thing for a Bible teacher.

And it's not like the fear would pop up just here and there, or just every now and then. Every single day, at every single turn, no matter where I was or what I was doing, I was tormented by this urgent sense of *Get Me*

Outta Here! I was up all night, then down all day, fighting back tears and sweaty palms and a racing heartbeat. For the first time in a long time, I seriously questioned my calling and my capabilities. You probably wouldn't believe how close I came to just quitting everything—whatever it took to make this awful feeling go away.

But God wouldn't let me. On separate occasions over the course of two months, He gave a few of my friends some very specific insight and discernment into me and my situation. You'd have thought they'd bugged my house and were listening in to every single prayer. They knew so much about what I was facing—and knew it in such eerily accurate detail—there wasn't much else I could do but listen when they came over and started talking. He ignited their tongues with words from heaven that spoke right to my heart. Their voices, His thoughts.

And then they prayed. Oh man, how they prayed! Not those warmed-up, leftover, mamby-pamby repeat prayers from the day before. These were the kind of prayers you can feel burrowing into your soul as each word penetrates those spiritual depths where the enemy tries to grab hold. These were prayers on fire. I walked away from each encounter leaving a trail of smoke curling up behind me. In Jesus' name, those friends commanded me out of my fear, and commanded the spirit of fear out of me.

And just like that *(snap!)* . . . it left. It really had no choice.

I'm not saying I still don't have to work hard to keep it in check. I'm actually standing guard against it right this very minute, shooing its creepy fingers off my keyboard while I write to you. But no way is that thing taking hold of my heart again, because as sure as I'm sitting here, I know when I felt the spirit of fear lift off me and run for its life, with the sizzle of those prayers hot on its tail.

I was healed. Whole. Set free.

It was done.

. . . .

Jerry and I were looking for a place to call home for our family and our ministry all together in one spot. We'd searched for property but hadn't found what we needed or what we could afford. Not on *this street*, at least. Yes. *This one.* We could have settled for a feasible option in another neighborhood a couple miles away, but for some reason I felt like we were supposed to be *here*. Prayed long and hard about it, yet I didn't see how it could happen . . . until one day . . . When. It. Just. Did.

I was driving past a house I'd ridden by for three years (including as recently as the day before) when I spotted the sign in the front yard. It couldn't have been there for more than ten or twelve hours. And in my mind I could see our name scrawled across it in bright pink writing. Where it said "For Sale," I was almost certain it also said "For the Shirers."

The sellers wanted out, and we wanted in.

I was so happy and excited and content. And yet there were reasons why, as perfect as it seemed, it wasn't exactly right for us. It still didn't have enough room for our ministry operation. After we bought it, we were forced to run our office out of a small bedroom and let our staff work from home till we could figure something else out.

Little did we know, however, that our new property was attached to another piece of land that already contained existing office space—and an owner who, two years later, would offer us the land and buildings for less than half of what he'd been trying to sell it for originally.

Less. Than. Half.

I'm not making this up. That's just how it happened. *It was done.*

Instantaneously. Inexplicably. Unbelievably. Not because we're so smart or had planned so strategically, but just because . . .

God is able.

. . . .

We like to travel with our children regularly when ministry calls us on the road. We've been to Australia. London.

Cape Town. Too many U.S. states to name. It's humbling and it's a privilege. But, wow, is it expensive! And once the kids moved past two years old—when their airline seats were no longer free—we weren't sure how to manage. Still aren't, really. We love for them to be able to see new places and to catalog these unforgettable experiences together with us as a family. But we also love being able to buy groceries, right?

Just recently, when looking at the prices of everything and comparing them against our budget, we didn't see how we could afford the expense anymore of all five of us jumping on a plane very often like that. Our only option, really, was to start declining invitations and curtailing our travel so our family could be together—which is where we all wanted to be. And yet a steady, fiery, divine calling kept rising in my heart and in Jerry's heart. We knew the Lord was commissioning us to go . . . and to stay with our family at the same time. What to do?

Enter God.

We were out of the country at a particular conference when a stranger—listen to me now—a man from Singapore we'd never met before in our lives, leaned over to us and asked if we were employed by a church or if we were just in itinerant ministry. We told him we're happily active members of our local church but are not on its payroll.

That was the entire conversation. *Nice meeting you, too, sir.*

But before the night was over, that man handed us a check written for an amount steep enough to cart all five of us Shirers halfway around the world and back.

My mouth was agape. So was Jerry's (and trust me, his mouth doesn't drop open like that very often).

Again, *it was done.*

Covered. Handled. Miracle.

Sure, we've got future trips to figure out, but you'd better believe we'll have a different outlook moving forward. Why?

Because God is able.

He keeps proving it time and time again.

. . . .

I could go on like this with amazing stories of the way God has changed our circumstances, the way He's changed *me.* And to be clear, I could also give you an equally long list of times when He has *not* answered me exactly how I'd requested and I've been left feeling disappointed, confused, and unsure.

Just because God *can* doesn't mean He *will.*

But just because He *hasn't* doesn't mean He *won't.*

The bottom line is that He is *able.* And because He is able, and because He is love, our hearts are completely secure in every situation, no matter how desperate or chronic or time-sensitive.

So as you start making your list, I don't want you to limit your range of *Its* to the obvious and external: unemployment, marriage problems, rebellious children, medical test results, compulsive addictions, looming bankruptcy. Sometimes His greatest miracles arrive not in the form of dollar signs and clean X-rays but in transformed attitudes and an abundance of unexplainable peace. Sometimes His best work is not what He does *for* us but what He does *inside* us. And believe me, that is no consolation prize.

Like when He changes a perspective.

Or refuels a lost passion.

Or refocuses an ignored, misplaced priority.

Or refreshes a spirit darkened by depression.

Or softens a heart grown cold and unforgiving.

Or exposes and transforms an impure, impertinent line of thinking.

It's not as spectacular and showy perhaps as a last-minute home buyer showing up on your doorstep, or a couple at church handing you the keys to a car they've decided to give to you instead of trading in. But it's some of the most amazing work He does. And from all the attempts we've made to change our hearts over the years, we should know!

If it was so easy to conquer that stubborn streak of ours, or to calm our temper, or to yank out that worrying gene—if *we* were the ones who were able—we would surely have fixed it all by ourselves a long time ago.

When God surprises you by changing your husband's mind, reorienting your child's direction, softening your boss's heart, or just brightening that no-hope look in your eyes, you can be sure He's been up to something incredible, inconceivable, borderline impossible.

That's because God is able.

I've watched a girlfriend of mine, for instance, go from wanting nothing at all to do with adoption to wanting nothing else more dearly. For years she's struggled with not being able to bear children, and frankly she's held God responsible for not giving her what she wanted—what everybody else seems to have. The constant frustration of tossing another negative pregnancy test in the trash can, coupled with the financial strain of turning to medical methods for assistance in the conception process, has caused as much strain on her marriage as on her body.

Adoption was obviously something she knew was there. Available. Yet even with a godly heart and a genuine desire for His will and plan, she just couldn't seem to go there in her thinking. Was it so wrong of her to want to be pregnant, to experience the indescribable bond of giving birth to her own child, to bring that new son or daughter home from the hospital, trying to determine if he or she had his daddy's build or her mama's expression?

But ask her today, and she'd tell you God has answered her prayer in a most unexpected but no less exciting fashion. Sure, the yearning for a positive pregnancy test is still there, but so is a heartfelt desire for that yet unknown child in another part of the world toward whom God is already knitting her affections. What she once considered distasteful and depressing now electrifies her with joy, surprise, and anticipation.

God has changed her heart.

Because God is able.

In fact, I'm more and more convinced that when He chooses to perform physical miracles in our lives—when He does what we consider supernatural and extraordinary—His chief intention even then is not to blow our minds but to cause our hearts to become more inclined toward Him and aligned with His. He wants us to trust Him, believe Him, and expect Him, until our primary goal is not that He answer our prayer exactly the way we've been praying it, but that we know Him more fully and intimately.

And when that change happens . . .

It's done.

I mean *really* done.

In a "once and for all" kind of way.

So the floor is yours now. You're my coauthor here. Tell me what brings you to this book. (I've left a little room below for you to write, if you like.)

Let it all hang out, right here at the beginning. Then when you're ready to turn the page, let's get to it.

. . . to your *It*.

_____

_____

_____

_____

_____

_____

_____

_____

CHAPTER 1

Time

"Now . . ."

Some things are just hard to describe. You search your brain for the right word, but you can't seem to find it.

Like trying to explain the view from high atop a snowcapped mountain peak. Or a particularly moving worship service. Or a late autumn sunset at the end of a peaceful day of vacation, silhouetting the bare tree branches with deep pinks and purples. Or the first bite of molten chocolate lava cake—or the *last* bite, for that matter.

Sometimes we're speechless. Nothing comes out. Then other times we run at the mouth, hoping the mere act of inhaling and exhaling might eventually catch up to that word our mind is chasing in the background.

Then sometimes we're like the apostle Paul who, when lost in amazed wonder of what he was trying to communicate, took to writing.

Perhaps none of his New Testament works is a better example of this than his letter to the Ephesians, which some scholars consider to be the pinnacle of all his writings. Go back and read it yourself. See if you can't hear him grasping and lunging for just the right words. He nearly runs out of breath trying to portray the greatness and grandeur of God, the vast scope of His wondrous acts, the hugeness of His love, and the wealth of our inheritance in Christ. Yet as beautiful as the wording is, as much spiritual ground as he covers, you still get the sneaking impression that human language simply does not have the descriptors for some of what Paul is wanting to say.

In the first half alone—a bit more than sixty verses— he takes us to *heavenly places* that stretch *far above all rule and authority and power and dominion*. He travels back in time *before the foundation of the world*, then zooms us forward to a future so rich with *eternal purpose*, it comes complete with an *inheritance* reserved under our name and with *all things in subjection under [Jesus'] feet*.

Somewhere in there, he awakens us from being *dead* in our sins—*strangers, separate, excluded, aliens*—to being made *alive together with Christ*, having the grace of God *lavished on us* for no other reason than *the kind intention of His will.* He tells us of a divine love that not only runs the *breadth and length and height and depth* of our wildest imagination but actually makes it possible for us to be *filled up to all the fullness of God*—right here in these tired ol' bodies of ours.

That's some extravagant language to describe God's extravagant power and love. These were the best words Paul could find to complete his enormous prayers, praying that our hearts would be thoroughly enlightened, that we would somehow grasp the riches of God's mercy and the grand hope of His calling, that we would see everything that's been made available to us in Christ, everything we've been given access to.

But he's just warming up.

Because right there in the middle of this stunning recounting of God's glory and grace, Paul hits us with one sentence so powerful, it is almost too much to bear: chapter 3, verses 20 and 21.

> Now to Him who is able to do exceeding abundantly beyond all that we ask or think, according to the power that works within us, to Him be the glory in the church and in Christ Jesus to all generations forever and ever. Amen.

It's a device known in ancient literature as a *doxology*. A majestic declaration of praise to God. An outpouring of divine honor. Sort of a gushing burst of worship that puts an exclamation point (or two . . . or three . . .) at the end of all this breathtaking stuff Paul's been talking about up until now.

It's a crescendo.

Crashing cymbals.

The big moment.

The cherry on top.

There are only a handful of these doxologies in all the Bible. And honestly, if we wanted to end this book right here on this page and simply bask in the colossal, comforting, confidence-building words of this one glorious statement, we'd probably be good for the rest of the week. Once you hear these two verses, the only thing left to do really is just worship and go home.

See if it doesn't strike you that way. I've printed it again in case you zipped past it too quickly before. Say it slowly, audibly, and deliberately. Let it speak directly to you and to your *It*.

Remember now—s-l-o-w-l-y. Drink it in. Savor it. Believe it.

Now to Him who is able to do exceeding abundantly beyond all that we ask or think, according to the power that works within us, to Him be the glory in the church and in Christ Jesus to all generations forever and ever. Amen.

And, if you can believe it, it gets even better—more rich and full—when you read it in other translations.

- ✛ to Him who is able to do far more abundantly than all we ask or think (ESV)
- ✛ above and beyond (HCSB)
- ✛ infinitely more (NLT)
- ✛ immeasurably more (NIV)
- ✛ [or as one of my all-time favorites puts it] God can do anything, you know—far more than you could ever imagine or guess or request in your wildest dreams (MSG)

It's indescribable.

And to this God be the "glory . . . forever and ever."

Amen? Yes, amen.

Any way you slice it, in whatever language or translation you may read it or hear it said, the core of it remains the same: *our God is able.*

And if we didn't believe it after reading the first half of Ephesians, we sure ought to believe it by the time we get to these final knockout verses. Because when we start viewing whatever may be worrying us against the backdrop of this One whose plans and purposes have been set in place for aeons, whose authority outranks every power structure known to man or even to the entire spiritual underworld, whose promises are ground-in deeper than—(sigh)—the grass stains on my little boy's *brand new* blue jeans . . .

. . . well, our *Its* suddenly don't sound quite so scary anymore.

Why? Because "God can do anything, you know."

He sure can.

God is able.

Mission Impossible

The other night we had pizza for dinner. (Don't judge me. Sometimes pizza is all I can manage.) And for reasons known only to the mysterious mind of a boy, my youngest grabbed his too-big slice of pepperoni pizza by its doughy handle of crust and lifted it up vertically from the box. Over his lap. Just for fun, I guess. It only took a split second for all those warm, melted toppings to slip and slide off the gooey crust and land with a messy plop, right in his lap.

Ha, ha.

He laughed. I didn't.

Not because I was upset with him (well, I was a little bit), but mostly because I strangely found myself hypnotized by that upside-down slice of pizza, dangling there in midair in front of his grinning face. Quick as a wink, I could already see how this "grab-the-paper-towels" image from the Shirer supper table was going to help me clean up a point I need to make right here in this first chapter.

I'm serious.

As we prepare to start digging into the heart of these two verses, I want you to think of them as an inverted triangle—with the small point or tip on the bottom, and the rest of it angling outward and upward into the air. Tiny at the base, big at the top. Just like an upside-down pizza slice. Got it? This is the way Paul arranged his thoughts in these verses—one small layer being the foundation for the next larger one.

I feel confident as we go along and you're holding up these verses to look at them in this way, a bunch of divine goodness is going to slide right off into your lap. But that's okay—because that's the kind of stain that will look really good on you.

So . . . got your piece of pizza? See that tip at the bottom? The place where you'd take your first bite? We're going to start there and tuck the very first part of the verse inside that little pointed nook. Just the first word of the verse for the moment, and then we'll watch the whole thing grow larger and more developed as it builds. One bite at a time. One layer on top of another. It's the one idea that fits snugly into the tip of that inverted pizza slice—the first word in the whole doxology.

The word *now*.

The reason we need to concentrate so hard on this first bite—the first word—is because our thoughts are usually all over the place.

Backwards.

Forwards.

What if.

What next.

How come.

Where to.

Why not.

But if you and I can just quiet down for a second, give our runaway minds a short break in the action, we may just feel God blowing away the clutter of our confused mental state, leaving us with one simple idea to focus on.

Now.

Get everything out of your head except *now*.

I understand that the current conditions in your life may not be your favorite thing to dwell on right *now*. You may have become very adept at concentrating on *later,* distracting yourself with the possibilities of the future. You may have grown accustomed to looking the other direction, daydreaming your life away, too overwhelmed at this point to even try figuring out solutions anymore for your present reality.

Or maybe there is no one big, hairy problem that's presently eating at you. (If that's the case, please know I'm happy for you. A bit jealous . . . but happy.) Maybe it's just the accumulated stress and strain from a long season of steady struggle.

Or maybe you aren't overwhelmed at all. More like *under*whelmed—bored with the sameness and mundaneness of a life you thought would be filled with so much more adventure. The predictability, the pointlessness. Urgh. You so desperately want a change, or at least a little excitement along the way. Maybe your contributions are being overlooked at work or at church, and you're craving the opportunity to put your best gifts forward, to show what you can do, to be involved in the kind of things you feel like you were placed on this earth to do.

No matter your current reality and the circumstances that describe it, there is a time to start connecting it all with God's infinite and indescribable ability. And that time, my pizza-stained friend . . . is now.

Look at your watch. *Now.*

Check the calendar date. *Now.*

Where are you standing? *Right now.*

Paul used this little bitty adverb as a tiny connector between that huge, blue ocean of vocabulary he'd been pumping out for three chapters, and the tightly packed dynamo of this one-line doxology. *Now* is the link between the impossible and the possible. The unmanageable and the divinely do-able. In light of all that other stuff God has already accomplished—a whole eternity's worth of wisdom and planning, of insurmountable odds and ultimate victory—here's the moment we've all been waiting for.

Now.

What does your *now* look like?

And what is the *It* that it's sharing space with?

Is it piled high with bills you don't know how you're going to pay? Is it littered with doubts about whether your marriage will survive until the next anniversary? Is it polluted by a particular sin or habit pattern that you absolutely hate in yourself but can't seem able to break free of? Or is it just a season marked by the humdrum rhythm of more normalcy than you ever wanted?

Does *now* hit you with a stabbing pain in your side every time you move a certain way? Does it cram your schedule so full, you rarely find the bed before midnight

or later? Does it contain a person who so completely mis-
understands you, nothing you say or do seems able to
change their mind and see the truth?

Whatever it is, this is when God's Word works. In real
time and space. Right smack-dab in the middle of your
now reality.

Oddly, however, we tend to disconnect the two—our
current reality and God's present ability. Somehow we
overlook the nearness of God when we are caught up
in the rhythm of life, dancing to the drumbeat of our
personal issues. We stay too tired or angry or frazzled
to remember that God can work on our behalf *now*. We
think it's only for the pastor . . . or that church lady and
her flying hat. You know, people like *them*.

Not us.

Not this.

Not now.

Well, Paul wanted to bridge that gap, to bring an end
to the separation anxiety that leaves us feeling discouraged and overwhelmed, unseen and uncared for. So he
purposely, strategically, intentionally used a word whose
purpose in the Greek language was to connect what he
had previously said in chapters 2 and 3 with what he was
about to say in the verses you and I are concentrating on
together. So maybe if we back up a bit in the passage and

in time, we can get a more detailed look at what Paul was up to.

Despite how familiar the book of Ephesians may feel on those crisp Bible pages of yours, it was once a piece of smudged parchment circulating through the wealthy, commercial city of Ephesus in ancient Greece. The believers there would read it or would hear it read, then they would pass it along to others, perhaps even to churches in neighboring cities. And even though the date of its original writing was first-century AD, the people who were first exposed to it had their own *now* circumstance to contend with. And Paul took the time to spell it out for them clearly. They were being asked to do something, to believe something, to support something that everyone and his mother deemed impossible.

Yes, *impossible.*

As impossible as your husband watching a *Say Yes to the Dress* marathon.

As impossible as solving the Middle East peace crisis with a text message.

I'm talking about *impossible.*

The apostle Paul told them that Jews and Gentiles, age-old enemies in every conceivable aspect of the term, were no longer on opposite cultural planets. By virtue of the gospel—the peace and reconciliation to God they'd received through the Messiah's sacrifice—they had become a third race of people known as the "body of Christ." And their unity as believers was designed to show the world that if God could do *this*, He most certainly could do anything.

You need to understand that the very idea of Jews and Gentiles getting along, respecting each other, cooperating together—it just wasn't happening. The fissures ran too deep. The haughtiness and hostility were too ingrained. No one had ever run for office on a Jew-and-Gentile reconciliation platform. They hated the ground the other had walked on. Their aims and desires were mutually exclusive. By a country mile.

Until Jesus.

Jesus changed everything.

He *still* changes everything.

Through the life and death of the Messiah, a "mystery" race had been conceived—which is exactly what Paul calls it in Ephesians 3:3 and in numerous other places. God wasn't just wishing these sworn rivals could somehow sit down and figure out a way to play nice together. No, He just flat went ahead and "tore down the dividing wall of hostility" (Eph. 2:14 HCSB) that had stood between them for dozens and dozens of long, gray-haired generations. He wasn't *appealing* for peace but was *proclaiming* peace—"peace to you who were far away and peace to those who were near" (Eph. 2:16–17).

It was done.

The only thing left was for these people to begin accepting by faith that what God had already accomplished, they could actually apply, not because of their power but because of His. As impossible as it sounded for this long-standing feud to finally end in a truce—even more, for them to actually begin *loving* each other and seeing themselves as a united family—Paul declared this their new reality. He wanted them to bring all of their crises to all of God's power, then stand back to see what God could do.

And God did it.

And if God was able to do that—the ultimate impossibility in most of their minds—then would anything else remain that He couldn't do for them?

For you?

I'd call that a good question.

And part of the answer is condensed into that little three-letter connector that holds all your heartache, your sleepless nights, your fear, your frustration, your pain, your despondency, your fatigue, your shame, your impossibilities . . . your in-laws.

Paul wanted the early Christians to make the connection.

You need to do it too.

Now.

In Tight Spaces

There was more. The cultural climate of the early church was not the only difficult situation Paul intended to connect to God's present ability.

I mentioned before that these two verses, Ephesians 3:20–21, are what's known as a doxology. If you attend a more traditional church, you may sing the "Doxology" as part of your worship service sometimes: "Praise God from whom all blessings flow . . ." You know the one? Doxologies, for us, whenever they occur, usually happen in our Sunday best. With the organ playing. With the choir singing. With the oven timer or the crock pot clicking on at home. It's polished. Clean. Ordered.

Just delightful.

But Paul wasn't sitting in church or the synagogue when he filled the page with these words of uncontainable praise. Nope, he penned these words of worship while sitting on the cold-floor, cold-food, maddening reality of Roman confinement. House arrest. Guards at the door, preventing his escape. When he wrote this glorious sentence, he was under a sentence himself, probably for as much as two years. Locked up. Locked down. Imprisoned. For serving God.

That's why Ephesians is one of four New Testament letters that have been called "prison epistles." The same words that still inspire us today in our living rooms and classrooms and in comfortable chairs at the kitchen table were actually composed from the cruel confines of jail time.

So this is not just a doxology.

It's a *prison doxology.*

Wrap your head around *that* for a moment.

Don't equate this grand phrase of Scripture with a coat and tie, a lady's dress hat, a gleaming church building, and a well-fed preacher. No, these were not easy words for Paul to write or say. They represented something he couldn't see with his eyes in the darkness of his current, personal condition, where loneliness cried out and the walls closed in around the stifled stench of his stark reality. His *now* was bleak and dismal. And yet somehow a doxology bubbled up within his spirit until, unable to be contained, it burst forth onto parchment paper. Paul experienced and exclaimed the ability of God amid his limited mobility, the greatness of God amid his tightly trapped existence, the awesome presence of God amid his frustrating lack of freedom.

What kind of believer do you have to be to voice a doxology from within a tight space and a tense situation you really, really want to get out of?

The kind who knows that timing is everything. The kind who draws the connection between their current circumstances and the power of God, the way Paul chose to do it. The kind who leaves the mountain of crisis long enough to cross the sturdy bridge of faith that leads directly to God's ability. The kind who knows that if God has allowed it *now*, He must have plans to display His glory *now*. The kind of man or woman who knows that *right now* is the time God can act on their behalf.

The same kind that you have the potential to be— right now—even in your impossible circumstance.

Not a Minute Too Soon

John 10:10 is one of my favorite passages in the Bible. Maybe one of yours too. It talks about a thief who comes "only to steal and kill and destroy," set against the contrasting intention of Christ, who comes that we may have "life, and have it abundantly."

I think most of us believe in that truth. In theory. In the abundant, ever-filling, overflowing life that Jesus came to offer us. And we believe it's hopefully waiting out there for us—if we can ever get past this one bump in the road. Our *It*. If we can ever just put this circumstance behind us. If we can ever get to feeling better, or get the car paid off, or get the school year finished, or get steady work. So we're always looking for it *later*, after we lose weight or get married or . . . well, you fill in the blank.

But it turns out, abundant life is not something you experience when there are no impossible situations to deal with. Abundant life is what Jesus offers and His Spirit enables during the times when you're right in the *middle* of them. It's meant to be experienced when all is wrong around you while all is simultaneously, inexplicably, very right within you. It's the smile that creeps to the corners of your lips when God fills your heart with a peace that runs contrary to your reality. It's the sense of divine adventure that pulsates in your soul even while you're sitting in a square, gray cubicle punching numbers all day long.

As soon as you connect your current circumstances to your God, He raises a banner of hope in your heart and mind. As soon as you believe He can do this—that He is able—something called abundant life actually shows up, right in the middle of the dreariness.

And it all starts when you make the connection.

Your marriage may be hanging by a thread. *Make the connection.*

Your finances may be a disaster. *Make the connection.*

Your child may be living a reckless, rebellious lifestyle. *Make the connection.*

Your doctor may have shown you an X-ray you never wanted to see. *Make the connection.* Your God is here. Your God is able.

And *now* is when you need to believe it.

Well, do you? You should.

Because *now's the time* to get on with it.

. . . .

Now to Him who is able to do exceeding abundantly beyond all that we ask or think, according to the power that works within us, to Him be the glory in the church and in Christ Jesus to all generations forever and ever. Amen.

. . . .

CHAPTER 2

Turning

". . . to Him . . ."

The airplane cabin was almost completely quiet, except for the occasional clicking of a flight attendant's heels, responding to a passenger's call for hot tea or a pillow. Night had fallen across the vast expanse of sky somewhere between London and Johannesburg—at whatever point along that trajectory we were. And as my husband finished the last sip from his coffee and leaned back against the headrest, I turned to gaze out the window at the thick, velvety darkness, studded everywhere with tiny sequins of starlight. South Africa, a land I had visited only in imagination, would be alive under my feet by morning.

But for now, I was just enjoying *this*—nearly twenty hours of flying time. The chance to breathe long and deeply. To not be needed. To not be reachable. Just to . . . be . . . and to not be. All at the same time.

So I was lost in the silence and beautiful darkness as our plane continued to rise toward its cruising altitude.

And then, it happened.

At 3:48 a.m.

We burst through a layer of thick clouds and were suddenly washed in the full, stark sunlight of daytime.

What only moments before had been a black ocean of ink instantaneously erupted into a stream of sunlight on the other side of all that cloud cover, glinting off the plane's wingtips and blinding me with its striking brilliance. I instinctively raised a hand to cover my eyes, turning away while retinas and pupils busily calibrated their adjustments. People—sleeping people—began audibly stirring and grimacing, flicking down the shades on their oval windows, reaching for sleep masks to shield themselves from the invasion of light.

And that's when I noticed it: the time display on a digital clock near the front of the plane that was still set to the time zone of our departure city. The full irony of the scene playing out before me registered slowly at first, and then picked up speed as the Holy Spirit did His work in me.

3:48 a.m.

The middle of the night.

How backwards.

We were in full sunlight *here* . . . during some of the darkest hours of night *there*.

And as clearly as ever, I heard the voice of God whispering in my spirit, reminding me of something that's actually an every-night truth, as readily available on the ground as it is at 30,000 feet . . .

> Even the darkness is not dark to You, and the night is as bright as the day. Darkness and light are alike to You. (Ps. 139:12)

Turns out, even the darkest hours of the night have a bright side, after all.

Every single night of your life contains a 3:48 a.m. A very dark one, at that. And hopefully the one that awaits you tonight could jump up and down as hard as it wanted and still not budge you from a deep sleep. But I'd imagine the 3:48 marker on your clock has also backlit some other nights when you've not been sleeping at all. You counted sheep, watched a sitcom, and checked a few e-mails in hopes of inducing drowsiness. But instead, you just ended up staring into the pitch-black darkness. Your problems seem heavier at that hour. Your worries won't sit still. Regrets that often go unnoticed behind your daily routine and responsibilities come scampering out of their hiding places to remind you they're still very much around.

But as I learned high above the Dark Continent that one unusual night, it's not dark everywhere at 3:48 a.m. In fact, where God lives, it's not dark . . . ever. I guess the way you see that hour just depends on the perspective you have when taking it in.

Head Spinning

Now is the time to know that God is able. To connect your current reality with God's present ability. But in order to do that—in order to experience Him *now*, to burst through the cloud cover that's keeping you from catching the rays of His light—you need to make a deliberate decision to change your perspective. It'll require some action on your part, beginning with a simple choice to pivot your attention 180 degrees away from where you're typically accustomed to looking. Away from what's frustrating you. Away from what's frightening you. Away from what's stealing all your joy and confidence.

Away from the darkness, to look toward the light.

If we expect to see God's ability in the here and now, it will require a *turning*. And this turning, according to Paul, is a turning to God.

"Now . . . unto Him . . ."

People often think of turning to Jesus as being a bit too impractical in terms of spiritual advice. Turning to Jesus. Looking to Jesus. What does that really mean?

Well, see if this doesn't clear it up in your mind a bit . . .

Quit staring at your problems!

While we seem to find the concept of turning to Jesus a bit mysterious, we don't have any difficulty turning to our aches and pains and wants and lacks. They're often all we think about. We stare at them through the windshield when we're driving. We paint them on the back of our eyelids at night. We measure them, compare them, analyze them, dissect them. If our eye catches a headline that refers to them or a talk show that addresses them, we stop what we're doing to watch and read and listen and commiserate.

We can't get enough of them.

And they'll take all our energy and attention if we let them. Because they hate being ignored. They'll scream and squeal and pout and protest. They'll remind you what all could go wrong if you dare to overlook them. And when they're not pressing your anxiety buttons, they're pushing their load of candied addictions at you, offering the cheap wares they sell for the relief you crave.

Poor you.

Poor me.

I'll admit, I've sat down during Sunday services and have found my mind wandering back to my worries and concerns—even there, even in church, even after singing His praise and exalting His name. A friend a few rows back might notice my solemn expression, texting me to see if I'm all right. I see her message lighting up beside me. Glancing at it quickly, I put down my phone (since good Christians don't reply to texts in church, right?—although I do sometimes tweet in church . . . or Instagram . . . or, well, never mind). I look over to give her a simple smile of thanks, grateful for her concern. There I am, in the middle of God's people and God's presence, yet with my mind completely wrapped up in my circumstances—enough that a friend can see it all over my face, and God can certainly see it inside my heart.

Who's really getting my worship here? What am I lifting up as the most important, most defining thing in my life? To what am I giving the bulk of my time and effort and energy and attention?

Where am I turning?

To Him? Or to them?

To His ability? Or to this apparent impossibility?

One of my little boys was having trouble falling asleep one night. "I'm having these bad thoughts," he whimpered, "I don't know what to do." So I hopped out of bed—like mamas do—and stumbled into his room, sat down beside him. "Honey, just try to make yourself think about *other* things. Good things," I said, "like . . . like, Disney World. We're hoping to go there this summer as a family. Think about getting to see Mickey Mouse!"

"Nah, it's not working, Mommy."

"Yeah, well . . . you love ice cream. Why don't you think about how good that bowl of chocolate ice cream was that you had today? Would that help?"

He shook his head. No.

I wasn't getting through. Just getting sleepier.

"Uh . . . hmm . . ."

Burning low on ideas, I reached over and held him close, rubbing his little shoulder and arm through his pajamas, then gently kissed him on the forehead while trying to come up with a new strategy. But he beat me to it. "I know what, Mom," he finally said, breaking the silence and looking up into my eyes, "I'll just think about you."

Ohhh, my baby. He's gonna make some girl a fine husband one of these days. I'm just sayin'.

And with that, he laid back in my arms and went to sleep, as God's Spirit taught me a full-sized lesson right there in my kid's twin-sized bed: how a mind fixed on the right thing—the right person—can change everything.

When was the last time you just told your stuff to shut up and go to sleep, and then gave your full attention—deliberately and intentionally—to the living Lord? Your Father. Your caregiver. Your provider. And then laid back into the big, strong arms of Psalm 46:10 and got r-e-a-l-l-y still, just lying there "knowing that He is God."

Worshiping Him. Meditating on Him. Repeating His Word from the depths of your memory or choosing new passages to write down and post in strategic places where you'll run into them on a regular basis. Reflecting on His grace, His glory, His love, His mercy, His power, His might, His majesty . . . His ability. Fighting the low-level cloud cover that's blocking out what you're wanting to see break through into your life.

You can toss and turn as you fret about your situation, or you can turn "to Him." No, it won't make all your problems go away—just as that airplane's ascent didn't make those clouds disappear. They were still there. We were just on the other side of them—the side where the sun was shining, in a different time zone and space. Focusing on Him will turn your heart, mind, and body in the sole direction where all your help is coming from.

Watch Where You're Going

"Unto Him." What valuable words to pocket into your living vocabulary. Perhaps that's why Paul included it twice in his Ephesians 3 doxology—the most powerful of all prepositional phrases—one time in both verses.

"Unto Him . . ."

"Unto Him . . ."

Twice the chance you'll never forget it.

Because let's be honest, we are always turning somewhere.

More often than not, we turn to *others*—to our friends, our pastor, our family, our prayer group. And that's fine. That's helpful. But if that's all the turning we ever do, we're just piling on blankets without ever cranking the heat up. We're putting a Band-Aid on our forehead instead of taking an aspirin for the headache.

The very best our best friends can do is to sympathize with our troubles. They can cry with us, pray with us, keep their ears open for us, put in a good word for us. But they can't do what God can do. They're not *able* the way God is able. Sure, He can use our various support systems to give us a hug, an observation, or a piece of wise counsel, but He alone has the power to invert situations, revert conditions, and overhaul circumstances. He's the only one who can give us exactly what is best, who can know us all the way to the back wall of our hearts, and who can flow everything that touches us through the ageless wisdom of His will so we are constantly within His loving care and keeping.

Sometimes, on the other hand, we turn to *ourselves*. After all, that's what we're conditioned to do. To dig in and try harder. To do it without anybody's help. Or maybe we're just hoping nobody else will see the mess we've made until we've done our best to fix it. We don't want them to find out how much struggle goes on behind our smiling faces and our perfect families. But turning inward leaves us fully exposed to pride and confusion, to stilted perspectives and limited resources. We think we're doing what's best. We're trying not to bother anybody. But becoming overly introspective can cause us to slide into an abyss of discouragement as we carefully consider all the ways we don't seem to measure up.

Christianity was never meant to be so intrinsic. It is *extrinsic*. It is all about looking outward toward Jesus, not inward at ourselves.

Our enemy is the one who wants us focused on ourselves—on our humanity, frailty, and need. God, however, wants us focused on *Him*—on His deity, His ability, and His boundless power. He's never overwhelmed or put off by our problems. He's not bothered by us, by the concerns of our hearts or the needs in our lives, no matter how much or how often we turn to Him. In fact, if we *don't* turn to Him and lay it all down, we only succeed at resisting His ability to reach in and change this.

To reach in and change *us*.

So we need to watch our preferred tendency for turning only to *others*, or turning only to *ourselves*. But we also need to be careful about turning too easily and exclusively to our *junk*. To television, to the Internet. To movies, sports, and hobbies. To numbing wastes of time, if not to shameful lacks of self-control. Let's be honest, sometimes it's just easier to shop than to deal with our lives. A great pair of shoes or a snazzy new gadget from the (insert common red or green fruit name) store tends to deaden us to our reality, in exchange for a few very expensive moments. We trade our own complicated world for a fantasy world that's easier to decode, control, and star in. We hope that maybe our problems won't seem as bad when we come back to them. At least we'll have had a few hours off— with our new pair of red heels or our shiny new phone. Who can blame us for that?

But while turning to healthy recreation can be a good part of coping with difficulty, we can't ask a gripping TV series to minister to the heart of our troubled teen. We can't eat enough Mexican food to reheat the coolness that's descended on our marriage. We can't play enough computer games or follow enough celebrities online to satisfy what's missing or make up for what we've lost.

God alone is able. Turning *to Him* is the secret to finding wholeness and to seeing our situation reversed in Jesus' name.

Nothing really changes when all we do is talk to each other. We just leave the restaurant with ten dollars less than we had when we walked in. We go back to our business and try to remember where we left things off. But when God speaks—listen to me now—worlds come into existence! New things are created! Old things pass away!

Now is the time to start doing some turning. Not turning any which way you please, but turning completely and consciously *unto Him*.

Right Turns

Refocusing our attention onto God is a noticeably consistent theme in both the Old and New Testaments of Scripture. In place after place, this one action of His people led to courage, led to comfort, led to revelation and rescue.

Old Testament: When the Israelite spies were sent by Moses to scout out the Promised Land, they saw giants.

They saw danger. They saw large cities, strong enemies, impenetrable fortresses. But two of the spies—Joshua and Caleb—had their eyes on something else. They saw the promises of God, the truth of His word, and the certainty of His ability. "We should by all means go up and take possession of it," they declared, "for we will surely overcome it" (Num. 13:30).

The majority of the men, if they saw God at all, saw Him only through the filter of their difficult situation. But the other two saw their difficulties through the lens of God's power and glory. Instead of turning to run, they turned into heroes, and became household names of faith for a whole generation.

Because they turned to Him.

New Testament: Mary Magdalene came to the tomb of Jesus early in the morning "while it was still dark." Hopes gone. Life over. What she found, however, was even worse than the horror she'd already endured. The stone that had sealed Jesus' grave was now missing. Someone had stolen Him, it seemed. His body, already savaged and killed, was now apparently being subjected to even further indignities.

And so she wept. And felt the piling on of despair. She'd thought it had been so bad it couldn't possibly get any worse. And yet it did. It had. It was.

Maybe that's been your experience too.

Then Mary would understand you. Because whatever finality she had begun to make of Jesus' torture and death, she had now been robbed of even the common decency of closure. The angels in the white clothing, although surely a shock to her senses, didn't offer her any specific answers. Neither did this guy who appeared to be the gardener, standing there, not looking very busy. But as she gazed off into the perplexing, impossible distance, she heard that mysterious "gardener" say, simply . . . "Mary."

Wait! Her name only sounded that way when spoken by one Person. Could it be? Was He here? Was it Jesus? There was only one way to find out. So . . .

"She turned . . ." (John 20:16).

She. Turned. Around.

And her gaze brought her face-to-face with the brilliance and beauty of the risen Christ. A simple change of perspective changed her life—the same change of perspective that can change ours too.

"Fixing our eyes on Jesus" is what makes us able to "lay aside" all the weights and sins and added pressures so that we are able to "run with endurance," joyfully pressing ahead into a life that's sometimes admittedly difficult but not defeating. "Eyes on Jesus" is the Bible's proven antidote to growing weary, to losing heart, to giving up, to going down (Heb. 12:1–3). We may not yet see the solution in our minds, the answer to our prayers, or the money in our bank account, "but we do see Jesus" (Heb. 2:9 HCSB), and we know He is able.

Sky High

It was one of those days where television channels suspended all other coverage but the news. Some terrible tragedy had occurred, gripping the heart of the nation. And as I was driving that afternoon between one errand point and another, I happened to pass by a local church and saw an unusual sight in their manicured lawn.

The American flag had been lowered to half-mast in honor of those who had been devastated most personally by the events. It hung there limply, almost in shame and sorrow, looking weaker than usual. Less proud. Humbled.

But flying next to the Stars and Stripes was another flag on another flagpole. And this flag—the Christian flag—was still stationed at the highest position on the mast, all the way up to the golden knob at the very peak.

I'm sure it wasn't the first time these flags had flown from different heights, side by side like that, but it was the first time I'd ever noticed it. And the contrast startled me. It had me straining my neck as I drove past, struggling to keep my eyes on the road and on this striking imagery at the same time. The American flag was lowered, but the flag honoring our faith was not. And I couldn't seem to stop turning to see it.

Those flags made an enormous spiritual statement that day, one that I'm certain caused the demons in all of hell to tremble. Those flags said in vivid red, white, and blue what the Bible makes clear in black and white.

No matter what, God is still in charge.

So why are we so quick to lower our flag of allegiance and confidence in Him when life hits us hard? What causes us to keep our worries and concerns flying high—the wind-whipped flags of our circumstances and issues—while simultaneously yanking down His flag from its deserved, peak position?

We worry for our families, for our kids, for the kind of world our grandchildren will grow up in one day. We despair over the trends and the divorce rate and the trillion-dollar deficit. It's all too much, everywhere you look, everywhere you turn . . .

Well, no, not *everywhere* we turn.

Look to Him. Keep your pledge of holy allegiance intact. Continue believing in His sovereign ability. Stop limiting His power to a box that's much too small to contain His power. Keep the flag of your faith flying high.

No matter what, He is still in charge. All authority and power are still in His hand. So keep your head up and turned in the right direction.

Yes, turn and see . . . and believe.

. . . .

Now *to Him* who is able to do exceeding abundantly beyond all that we ask or think, according to the power that works within us, to Him be the glory in the church and in Christ Jesus to all generations forever and ever. Amen.

. . . .

CHAPTER 3

Truth

". . . who is able to do . . ."

I'm sure you've noticed, we don't live in the same world we grew up in.

That whole side of the street that was nothing but a big green field across from the neighborhood I used to live in? Now it's a shopping center complete with a drive-thru cleaners, a children's clothing consignment shop, a nail salon, and a place that sells fantastic chicken wings. (My sons couldn't be happier.)

The home mailbox that used to be for handwritten letters, shower invitations, and monthly magazines? Now it's mostly for bogus sweepstakes and credit card offers. And the technological advancement called e-mail—the one that made us lift our eyebrows in amazement when it first appeared on the scene—is quickly taking a backseat to ever-expanding ways of communication. Now we want to see each other's faces on screen while we chat.

It's just different. We're forced to adapt. Things change.

And while some of it is exciting and new, while we love being able to jot someone a quick text from the school pick-up line, while we're glad we don't need to drive clear across town to find modern conveniences, our souls do hunger for things we can count on, things that won't adapt or reinvent or change.

At least, I certainly do.

I like things to stay the way they are. Case in point: One Friday night nearly a decade ago, my son was staying over at Granny's house—(thank You, Jesus)—and my pleasantly adjusted plans for the evening included a quick swing by the video rental store for my favorite romantic, girlie flick, a cozy blanket on the sofa, and two hands cupped around a steaming, warm mug of fresh-brewed goodness. Ahh, take me away.

What I found instead, to my disbelief, was that our neighborhood video store had completely overhauled their stock since my last visit, replacing all of their VHS tapes with DVDs. Well, I didn't *own* a DVD player. And I had no intentions of buying one. But now, if I still wanted my blanket and my sofa and my two hours of film-induced escape, it was going to cost me $200 for a new piece of equipment that I didn't really want. I wasn't interested in the "new and improved." Our trusty VCR was in perfectly good condition even if it was becoming archaic.

Yup, sometimes we prefer things to just stay the same. Like the faithful love of a spouse. The innocence of childhood. Healthy skin. Reliable transportation. Gas pump and grocery store prices.

Yet as much as we may desire those, we don't always get them. And when we don't, our hearts can start to wonder if we can truly be assured of *anything* in life— anything besides change and loss and stress and more disappointment.

Good news: we can.

Oh, yes . . . we can!

No matter how progressive and postmodern our culture becomes, and no matter how many technological advancements take place, there is still such a thing as unchanging, unflinching, unadulterated truth. No matter what country you live in, what city you're from, what language you speak, or what you do for a living—real, solid truth maintains a constant balance at any elevation.

Two plus two equals four. Everywhere.

Gravity holds us to the ground. Everyone.

There are twenty-four hours in a day. Every day.

A snoring spouse is annoying. Every night.

(Well, it had to be said.)

So when Paul wrote the words that fill up this third tier in our inverted pyramid, he intended to declare an absolute, unconditional, irrevocable truth in a world overrun with constant change and relativity: God, he said, "is able to do" it.

When the Scripture declares God's power and might to be unlimited, unstoppable, and boundless, we are staring at a truth that's more certain than the fat grams in a doughnut, than the battery life on a sundial, than the chances of running into a cheapskate at a coupon convention.

God = Is = Able.

Any way you add it up.

This is something we can know for certain in our hearts right *now* in regard to the seemingly impossible situation we're facing. It is something we can keep *turning* our lives toward with confidence every minute of every day. He can do it. He is able. God has a raw ability and power potential that can take on your worst difficulties without even breaking a sweat. That's the *truth*.

Bank on it.

And honestly, this truth can transform your whole life, if you choose to believe it. When you are certain that *God can*, then even the most impossible, discouraging situations of your life become less threatening and ominous. You could be sitting right in the middle of a tornadic whirlwind of events, with everything spinning violently out of control all around you, yet still experience a deeply rooted sense of assurance because you know the truth—the truth of God's ability—the truth that never, ever changes.

God can.

But I do want to go ahead and deal right here with a question you're probably thinking, because I know I'm thinking it, and I've thought it many, many times before throughout my life. Perhaps you've been willing to follow me so far in this book, and you're doing your very best to turn the focus of your faith entirely toward God and His ability, despite your circumstances. But you still have a burning, real-life concern you'd like to ask: "Priscilla, if He *can* do it . . . then why isn't He?"

The tumor is still there.

My family is still in crisis.

My church is still without a pastor.

My grown son or daughter still can't find work.

The settlement for my flood damage claim is still hung up in some office building somewhere.

And . . . God is *able*?

Sure doesn't look like it.

I hope you hear what I'm about to say with the gentleness I intend, because if that comes close to describing the way you're feeling—trust me, I do understand. I've been there and thought it. But whether or not God CHOOSES to do something is a question of His *sovereignty*, not His *ability*. Whether or not He WILL do it is *His* business. But believing that He CAN—that's *our* business.

His ability is not what's in question. It never has been. Never will be. You must be willing to settle this truth in your heart once and for all.

But perhaps this leaves you with a second question, more disturbing than the first. You believe in His ability—His power—yet you question His *willingness*. You're wondering about His love, whether He even cares enough to help. And this question is understandably where a lot of people just quit trying and believing altogether.

But don't you quit. Keep on reading.

According to Scripture, this God who is "righteous in all His ways" is also "kind in all His deeds" (Ps. 145:17). Hear that? *Kind*. And while He may allow things into our lives that are decidedly not good, His Word promises He is still working all things together *for* our good in Christ (Rom. 8:28). His heart is brimming over with compassion and affection for you. He calls you the "apple" of

His eye (Deut. 32:10; Ps. 17:8 ESV), and is so endeared to you that He lifts His voice to sing songs over you (Zeph. 3:17). You are His "beloved" (Deut. 33:12; Rom. 9:25), and His "banner" over you is "love" (Song of Sol. 2:4). He is always willing to do what's in your best interest. He is constantly seeking to bring about the finest result in your circumstances, even though His methods are not always human-approved or understood. "No good thing does He withhold from those who walk uprightly" (Ps. 84:11). Not one thing.

So, no matter what we want our relationship with God and His actions toward us to be, it will always come down to a matter of trust—trusting that He is able and that His kindness toward us makes Him always willing in His infinite wisdom to do what is best. He can see more than we can see, and He can love us without needing to explain why His love needs to look like *this* at the moment.

Because the truth is, you and I—walking around so often with our heads down, our bristles up, our focus on the severity and heaviness of our problems—we have no idea the activity that God is currently orchestrating in our lives, not to mention the protective rescues He has already accomplished. The mere fact that you are still alive and holding this book in your hands means you have been spared some tragedies, you have been shielded from certain evils, you have been steered clear from who knows how many dangerous people and situations that could have done you in by now. God may have healed you of sicknesses you didn't even know you were carrying around. He may have rectified circumstances on your behalf before you were even aware you had a problem.

He has *already* been working behind the scenes of your life.

He always is.

Wonder what God has already done for you *today* without even telling you? (And without being thanked for it?)

What if you and I knew He was planning to bring about a big change in our *It* circumstances, but that He knows the best time for us to see it all coming together is still six months out? Wouldn't we want to be patient and wait for His absolute best?

You can either be upset that He hasn't brought you a job *now*, or you can choose to stay patiently excited that the job He's already planning to bring you *later* will pave the path toward your destiny.

You can walk out on your marriage now, or you can determine to rest while the small seed of restoration that's already stirring in your spouse's heart erupts later into a volcano of rekindled love and passion. Sure, *now* seems better. But not if any "now" solution wouldn't come with the full-blown blessings benefit package that God is already intending to give you in time, in His perfect way, and in His infinite wisdom.

Just because you can't see it or feel it or tell your friends about it right now means only one thing: not that He's unable, but that His sovereign love is acting right this moment out of sight and without your knowledge. Because His love (as Psalm 136 says) is eternal. Way bigger than just right now. And being willing to trust this truth is part of what believing in His ability is all about.

Is God doing what you want Him to do today? Maybe not. Is trusting Him to take action making you feel like a superstitious fool? Maybe so. But you cannot out-ask, out-pray, out-dream, or out-believe in the willingness and ability of God. The Father's ability to give to us exceeds our ability to ask. And when your heart is set on this *truth*, you're standing on a fact that will never change in a highly changeable and challenging world. It will help you sleep easier, laugh harder, and live more peacefully in the midst of trying times.

So as hard as it is to deal with whatever it is you're enduring, you are walking in 100 percent truth when you turn your heart, mind, and spirit all the way toward God's ability. This posture puts you in the most receptive position of all with which to watch Him at work.

Explosive Truth

Paul fully understood how life on the cloudy side of God's sovereignty could feel. But he also knew the prevailing, persistent truth of God's ability. And that's the place where he kept his attention locked like a laser.

After being blinded on the Damascus Road by a light brighter than the Texas sun in August, Paul was later imprisoned, then miraculously freed. He was beaten to within an inch of his life, yet survived, full of joy and gratitude. He was shipwrecked on a dark, stormy sea, only to be spared to continue serving his Lord. And here he was again—in prison, writing this letter to the Ephesians—still focused on the delivering ability of Almighty God.

Over and over, Paul had experienced this truth: *God is able.* And he had lived with it long enough and faithfully enough that when he chose the word to describe it, he employed the Greek verb *dunamai*—a word that sounds suspiciously like an English word we've adapted almost directly from it.

The power of God that fuels the truth behind His ability is no thin, flimsy, ninety-pound-weakling kind of power. Unh-uh. It can be explosive. *Dynamite* like. And while this English word is not an exact translation of the Greek word that Paul used, I can't help but see a hint of illustration here. God's is a power that, if drilled into the depths of your most impossible problem, can blow a hole in it so massive, you could drive a Mack truck through it. When solid rock is touched off by dynamite power, the truths of physics take precedence over everything else, no matter how stubborn or stony the obstacle. The presence of explosiveness thwarts all other objectives. It will do what it will do, and the pieces will fall where they may. But whatever they do, they cannot stay the same. When God demonstrates His power—*ka-pow!*—change is nonnegotiable.

God's *dunamis* (the noun form of His power) can cause things to explode (like the demand for your product or business). It can rearrange things (like your loved one's passions). Flatten things (like your most difficult stronghold). Restructure things (like your floundering financial portfolio). Lift things (like that looming cloak of depression). And produce things (like the perfect fifth-grade teacher for your child). Your most pressing issues don't stand a chance of resisting, not when God's power shows itself.

So do you need a fiery, explosive, steel-crushing, mind-bending, life-altering miracle to change something in your life?

Well, dynamite. The God you serve has resurrection power, the effects of which can have sudden, earth-shattering results. And honestly, it's a power that no human illustration can really scratch the surface of accurately explaining.

God has the ability to transform the whole shebang—emphasis on the *Bang!* It can happen in a flash, or it can happen with slow burns of steady change. But those problems that keep you up at night and interrupt the flow of your daily life can't do anything that's beyond the reach of God. His ability is your dynamite. You're in the right place, and you've got the right God.

He can do it—for you—because He is able.

For Me?

I grew up in church from, I guess, somewhere around the week I was conceived. Preacher's kid. The number of Sundays and Wednesdays (and a whole lot of other days too) when I wasn't in church as a little girl could probably be counted up with only the number of coins in your pocket or purse right now. As a result, church has always been a place and culture I've known extremely well, from day one.

I did children's Sunday school. Vacation Bible School. Won the sword drill a lot (which was more a testament of my need to impress people than of my consecrated love for God and His Word). I drove my teachers absolutely bananas, because I knew the answer to everything . . . or at least I thought I did. *Does anybody else here know the answer besides Priscilla? Anybody?* I didn't give them many chances to find out. If my teachers had taken weekly votes, I'm sure I would've swept the awards for "most annoying student."

And while that's a really good way to grow up—in church and with good Bible teaching—I've got to admit something: I wasted a lot of years merely having a lot of Bible information cataloged in my head, but without always understanding one very basic Bible fact—that God's promises were not only truth for everyone in general, for everyone else. They were His truth for *me.*

Listen, I've gone into a lot of situations in my life scared to death or paralyzed by so much insecurity that I never even gave some things a shot. I've churned up a lot of ground spinning my wheels and going in circles. I've spent a lot of days reeling from mistakes and missteps, sure that I'd ticked God off bad enough this time that I wasn't getting back into His good graces for a good long while. And those things happened because I hadn't personalized God's Word. Sure, I *believed* it, but I didn't believe it for me. All of that stuff I knew and could quote word-for-word to people? I thought it was exactly what God had in mind for them and their life and their own situation. But I didn't necessarily believe it was for me or for mine.

So while I was praying the roof down in Bible studies and Bible classes and in people's homes when we got together for things like that, I didn't always feel like I should trouble God with some of the heavier matters I was up against personally. After all, He might not answer me. Or He might answer me with a solution I didn't want to hear. Or He might be far too busy with other important matters. In my mind, His work was for other people, for other stories and testimonies, not mine. Why should I expect God to do that for me? What had I done to deserve those same blessings? He didn't have time for me and my little old problems.

What a waste it was for me to think that.

What a waste for any believer to think that.

If you can identify with me, hang on—because Ephesians is ready to usher both of us right out of this hollow, impotent, spiritual lie and into abundant living. Look at the common thread in Paul's prayer that leads up to the doxology.

- ✛ "that He would grant *you*" (3:16)
- ✛ "that Christ may dwell in *your* hearts" (3:17)
- ✛ "that *you* . . . may be able to comprehend" (3:17–18)
- ✛ "that *you* may be filled" (3:19)

All that Paul had been discussing was deliberately focused on the church and the unique, diverse individuals it comprises. He wanted those believers then, and us now, to refuse to live detached from God as if we are just faceless people in a very large crowd. This is the special, personal connection that rolls out the red carpet for verse 20. So in this verse, the phrase "He is able to do" isn't generic and impersonal. It carries an application to all believers, as if a little parenthetical statement is hanging out there on the end of it. Take a look:

"Now unto Him who is able to do . . . [for us] . . ."

For us = For me and *for you*!

Collectively, yes. But also individually and personally.

I should've trusted that all along.

And so should you.

Like the greater church of Ephesus that Paul was addressing, you and I as individual believers make up the greater church today as well. And God "is able to do" for *each* of us—personally, directly, intimately. Now we just have to believe it.

Because what good is a child's belief that his parents have enough food in the house unless he also is confident there's enough food *for him*? How does an employee derive any benefit from knowing her company has enough resources to pay salaries for the coming year unless she believes there's enough *for her*? What's the use of a wife knowing her husband is a dependable and faithful human being unless she believes his faithfulness also extends *to her* and their relationship?

Knowing God's gifts are *for you* changes everything.

One of the ways God made this truth so remarkably clear to me recently was while I was reading the Gospel account of Jesus' miracle at the wedding in Cana, found in John 2.

You probably know the story. Jesus and His disciples had all been invited to the big event. His mother, Mary, was there as well. And at some point during the celebration and festivities, the wine that was being served to the guests in attendance ran out. Not good.

Mary tickles me. She sort of ignores Jesus' comment that He wasn't yet ready to display His power, not in this way at least. She turns to the servants and tells them, "Whatever He says to you, do it." *My boy will take care of this.* And He did. He told them to go fill up the jars with water, all the way to the top, and then to skim out a taste for the chief steward to sample.

As you recall, the water had miraculously been changed into wine by the power of God—a better wine, in fact, than what they'd been pouring before. And *then*, the Bible says, "His disciples believed in Him" (John 2:11). *Then.*

You mean, these guys—these "disciples"—weren't believing in Jesus before? Not until just now?

This can mean only one thing: that it's possible to be a "disciple" and not "believe." It's possible to bear the disciple label—to learn of Him, to walk with Him, to pray to Him, to serve Him, to sit on that pew Sunday after Sunday to worship Him—and yet still not really trust Him with your life and all the circumstances in it.

Sadly, there are way too many disciples of God whose trust in Him doesn't extend beyond the churchy thoughts they know are supposed to be in their head, who don't operate as if His truth is a real thing. (Trust me, I'm not pointing any fingers.)

But, listen, believing in Jesus—I mean really trusting Him on a practical, daily level—is supposed to be real. It's supposed to work. It's supposed to transform us and make us different than before. We're supposed to "watch expectantly for the LORD," to "wait for the God of my salvation," fully confident with the biblical assurance of faith that "my God will hear me" (Micah 7:7).

Yes . . . me!

He "is able to do"—for you!

And even if it means waiting, even if we don't understand, even if His answer looks nothing like what we wanted or expected, the believing heart clings to what he or she knows—the *truth*—that the one who is Faithful and True is also willing and able.

. . . .

Now to Him **who is able to do** exceeding abundantly beyond all that we ask or think, according to the power that works within us, to Him be the glory in the church and in Christ Jesus to all generations forever and ever. Amen.

. . . .

CHAPTER 4

Transcendence

". . . exceeding abundantly beyond . . ."

Gotta tell you something—something I never thought I'd say.

Ever.

Here goes: I'm grateful for *unanswered* prayers.

I'm serious.

When I think back through the years to some of the relationships, desires, and ambitions I asked God for—*begged* God for—I am so grateful He chose not to answer my shortsighted prayers the way I was asking Him to.

Certainly wouldn't have said it back then—back when there were some situations that had me frustrated, impatient, and panic-stricken. Back when some things that were important to me at the time weren't panning out my way. But now, years down the line, far removed from the impetuous, impulsive experiences that were spurring me on to such urgent demands of Him, I can see more clearly. I can see that He was doing things *beyond* my wildest expectations—even in denying my requests.

Beyond.

That's the way He operates.

Exceedingly. Abundantly. Beyond.

He's always looking beyond the realm of our sight. He's always thinking beyond the scope of our thoughts. He's always mapping out a plan beyond the trajectory of our ambitions. He's always working out a miracle that *transcends* the farthest reaches of our imagination.

That's the way Paul describes the extravagant, profuse, exaggerated capacity and work of God in just these two little verses.

I love it.

And I am so grateful for it.

As we've journeyed together so far, we've already made some powerful, life-changing choices. We've decided to be *now* disciples, concentrating on God's present connection with our current life circumstances. We want to be people who keep our heads *turned* away from our fears, focused instead on our God. And we will not be detoured from the unchangeable *truth* of God's ability no matter what our circumstances look like. We're munching our way up this upside-down pizza slice of a Scripture, and we're starting to discover (or perhaps remember, for the first time in a long time) what true faith in Him actually tastes like. Plus, as an added bonus, that incessant growling in our stomachs—all the worry and dread and doubt and despair—is hopefully starting to die down and fade away, being drowned out by the lip-smacking power of a God-infused flavor explosion.

That's what happens when you get a revelation of God's ability.

And that's good.

This next bite, though, is sure to be the best one yet.

In fact, it's going to be "exceeding abundantly beyond" all expectations—which is amazingly how the Bible describes not only the extent of God's ability, but His ability *for you*—personally, intimately, individually.

Exceeding.

Abundantly.

Beyond.

As in, extra, extra filling and delicious.

When Paul started assembling the words that would ultimately become Ephesians 3:20, he could barely find the right verbiage to communicate this part. See him sitting there, his reedy pen poised in one hand over the parchment, the other hand pressed to his forehead, scanning his knowledge for every available word in the Greek language to get his point across. Maybe he tried one and then another. Writer's block. No one word was good enough, not when standing alone all by itself. Even the most extravagant word couldn't encapsulate all that he was trying to communicate. So it would need to be several words strung together then. Big words. Meaty words. Words that, by the time he finally built them up to where he wanted them, he was almost making up some new words to do it. Old ordinary words just didn't quite cut it. You can almost hear Paul tripping all over himself trying to explain the unexplainable.

Hyperekperissou hyper

Translation . . .

Exceeding. Superabundantly. Beyond.

Hyperlink

Once Paul figured out which combination of words would be the best he could manage, he still wasn't quite satisfied that they told the whole story. So twice within this little three-word chunk of Scripture, he tacked on a preposition that juiced up the words beyond their original meanings.

The particular prefix that did the job for Paul is a word form that's also familiar to us today. Look back and see if you can catch a glimpse of it in the Greek.

Hyper.

Let's stop and think for a minute about what "hyper" can do.

Hyper can turn ordinary car headlight bulbs into *hyper*-white headlight bulbs, the kind that can blind you in your rearview mirror and make you wish the car with the piercing brights behind you would either hurry up and turn off or just pull around you.

It can turn normally active children into *hyper*active children. And turn their mothers into ranting, raving lunatics. Or so I've heard. I couldn't say for sure.

(Ahem.)

It can take the natural extension of your knee or elbow and *hyper*extend it, until you're having to get an X-ray, a protective cast, and a few morning sessions of physical therapy.

There's the usual drive, and then there's *hyper*drive—a whole other realm of speed and acceleration. There's outer space and *hyper*space. Healthy tension and *hyper*tension.

So whenever "hyper" finds its way onto a word, it makes the original word bigger and grander, faster and stronger, deeper and more multidimensional than it was before. It's like putting those words on steroids. It's everything the base word says, and then some. Plus some. Takes it to a whole new level. Beyond.

When writing about God's ability to express power, Paul used this prefix twice. *Hyper hyper.* That's two levels of "beyondness" he wanted to communicate. (I think I made that word up. Just go with me on this.)

Not just beyond, but *beyond* beyond.

Not just way past, but *way past* way past.

That's how Paul describes God and His power to perform astounding miracles: *hyper*-able. *Transcending* the normal realm of ability. Way past whatever you'd already consider to be "way past."

And so I'm just wondering: When you think about the kind of miracle it would take to completely revolutionize your circumstances, to cleanse your conscience, to repair your relationships, to brighten your outlook, to dig you out of this hole you're in, what is the most amazing, mind-blowing, stupefying solution you can picture? What would be *way* past, way *beyond* your wildest hopes?

Go ahead, take a minute to get that resolution in your head.

Got it?

Well, guess what? He can do *beyond* that. "Exceeding abundantly" beyond it!

Way past your "way past."

When you really stop and think about it, this has always been His way. He's always been a God of abundance. Is there any reason other than God's "beyondness" that can explain why, when He decided to create water, He just went ahead and created whole oceans? Wasn't the intense heat and mass and splendor of a single star impressive enough all on its own? Did He really need to go and create entire galaxies, raging with billions and billions of stars, most of which no human eye will ever see?

Couldn't birds have just been yellow? Or black? In a standard size and shape? Why create thousands of different types and species? Big ones, little ones, cute ones, even funny ones. He didn't just make hills; He made the Rocky Mountains and the Himalayas. He didn't just make the sun; He made sunrises and sunsets.

He's just beyond the beyond.

Way past, way past.

Recently, I heard someone talking on the radio about how they did a little personal culinary experiment, seeing if they could spend an entire week eating only one color of food per day, based on the seven colors of the rainbow: red, orange, yellow, green, blue, indigo, and violet. Boring, but possible.

Strawberries and red peppers on one day, oranges and cheese the next, fresh lettuce and vegetables, blue corn chips and grape juice. But after a week of restricting themselves to this odd, monochromatic diet, the craving for multicolors and variety became overwhelming, as if they were being deprived of oxygen and water. When midnight finally rolled around at the end of their seven-day, self-imposed "fast," they desperately ordered a pizza with every color topping they could think of, so they could eat it all at once.

That's because God, being so rich in abundance, has trained our own hearts for abundance. For shapes and textures. For clears and solids. For things that are supple and things that are firm. We really don't know any other way to interpret life except through His astonishing variety and creative wonder.

We call it normal. Like it's nothing. But that's because the only world we know—this extraordinary planet and universe—has been spoken into existence by a God who is "exceeding abundantly beyond" in every detail. Yeah, He just spoke it, and it was there. Imagine that! So why should we expect His ability at work in our lives to be any less incredible?

He's just beyond.

He's way past our way past.

Beyond Beyondness

I want to be sure you get the picture so an image of God's "beyondness" is seared into your mind.

Behind our house is a fairly steep drop-off that tumbles downhill into a creek bed. It's rural and beautiful, and it's part of what tugged our heartstrings toward this little place out here with its peace and quiet and room for three rambunctious boys. But I've got to admit, the clanging bells on my mama-sense went into high alert when I realized how steeply that hill crashes down directly behind the area where my sons run and play and (Lord, help me) burn off that wild energy of theirs in the afternoons.

So actually, one of my very first orders of business before we even moved in was to string up a simple chicken-wire fence across that natural ledge, giving them (if nothing else) a visual reminder of where the boundary limits are. I've told my boys that the fence is the limit. They can do pretty much whatever they want back there—climb stuff, chase stuff, roll around in stuff, eat stuff—but don't ever let me see them back behind that creekside barrier I've put in place. Not one single step *beyond*.

We've made this expectation very clear.

Both in their ears and on their rears.

So if I happened to be sitting at my dining room table one day, reading a book or wondering what I might throw together for supper tonight, and I looked up and saw one of my little boys clear across on the other side of the creek, I would immediately recognize that his soon-to-be sore bottom had taken him way past *my* way past. *Beyond* the expectation. He'd be in big trouble for going *beyond* my limits.

But I'll tell you what: he'd be in even bigger trouble if the phone rang while I was sitting there, and my neighbor who lives up behind me—beyond the tree line, where I can't even see her house in the spring and summertime for all the thick brush—was calling to ask if I was missing a son . . . a son who was now several acres distant from his back yard, all the way over on her front porch, relaxing and sipping a glass of sweet tea like he's a grown man who pays his own bills and doesn't have to answer to anybody.

(I digress.)

That would mean he was even farther *beyond* my expectation than he had been before. Not just *beyond*, but *beyond the beyond*.

Can you see it?

That's just a little picture of what God means when He says He can go way past our way past. *Beyond* our *beyond*.

Or imagine you and your spouse had been away for the weekend, and you left your high-school senior teenager at home alone to look after the house. All you asked, except for adherence to the usual rules and restrictions, was that by the time you got home on Saturday night, their messy room was to be picked up and put back in shape. That was the expectation you'd set—the bare minimum of what they needed to achieve before you returned. But when you pull into the driveway the next evening and step inside the door, you find that not only have they cleaned their room, they've straightened up the entire house. That's *beyond*. And honestly, you'd have been plenty satisfied with just that. But there's more. A bit of dinner is cooking on the stove, with the plates and silverware set out on the table. Even your own room has been vacuumed and dusted, the bed linens turned back, the scent of a steamy bath emanating from a candlelit bathroom.

That kid just went *w-a-a-y beyond* your *way beyond*.

Are you getting the idea?

One more, just to be sure.

Let me tell you about a girlfriend of mine whose husband is, uh . . . well, he's a great guy. He really is. Steady. Solid. A godly man. The kind of guy any parent would want his or her daughter to marry. But let's just say my friend's husband is a little challenged in the romantic department. Great husband—just not the gushy, mushy, gift-buying, hand-holding, public display of affection type. He's practical. Responsible. He might think a kitchen appliance would make a perfectly acceptable birthday gift. (And it *would*, if it were accompanied by a part-time chef.)

One year for her birthday, my friend told me she was just hoping for a sweet, endearing card from her man. Just a card. *To you, from me*, along with maybe a few sugary, thoughtful, applicable words, showing her that he (not his secretary) had actually read it before selecting. Didn't need to play a Lionel Richie song when she opened it. Didn't need to be in a big, extra-postage envelope. Didn't need a special cut-out that might hold a pass for a day spa appointment or anything. Just a straight-up "Happy Birthday" card with the customary, poorly rhyming poem inside. That would do it for her. That was her expectation. Shoot, this would have been *beyond* her expectation, given her husband's track record on her other birthdays.

And sure enough, he did it. When she got home on the afternoon of her birthday, a single card was propped up in the bed on her pillow. How nice.

But, hey, that wasn't all. Next to the card was a gift. In a thin, slender, oddly shaped box.

Surprise, surprise.

Her man had now gone *beyond* her expectations. Before even opening that gift, just the sight of it put a huge smile on her face. He was a good man! He really was.

She couldn't wait to open it.

Until she did.

An umbrella.

(Wah, wah.) Oh well, he tried.

But—but that's not important. He'd given it a shot. Good for him. He'd gone *beyond*. So she forced a little smile, eager to open her card. That's all she'd originally wanted anyway. That was her expectation. Even if all it said was . . .

"I hear it rains a lot . . . in Paris."

Ohhh, yeah.

Attaboy.

Exceeding.

Abundantly.

Beyond. Beyond.

Hungry for More?

We want to believe this is true. We want to believe in God's "beyondness." The issues we're facing, the challenges on our plate, the difficulties that strain our every muscle of willpower and then laugh at every attempt we make to deal with them—they *need* a beyond-beyond solution. They'll never go away without a way-past infusion of something only God could create.

So what are we waiting for? Why aren't we asking for that? Believing for that?

A young Christian college president, new to the job and eager to expand his fund-raising efforts, went to visit a major donor one day in hopes of securing a pledge for an additional gift. He was invited into the well-appointed office and was graciously given the opportunity to make his appeal, after which the gentleman reached for his checkbook, unscrewed the top from his fountain pen, and asked how much money they were talking about.

It's a question the new administrator probably should have asked himself before going in. But frankly, he was caught a little off guard by how quickly and easily the man had responded. After doing some fast figuring in his head, he scooted forward in his chair, cleared his throat, and gingerly announced a figure that he feared was perhaps a little too bold, given the situation and their first meeting and all.

The wealthy businessman nodded, looked down, saying nothing, then scrawled out a check for that precise amount, tore it loose, and handed it to the visitor across his desk.

Effusive thanks. Smiles and handshakes.

But as he was showing his guest out, the man put a hand on the school president's shoulder, looked him square in the eye, and said, "I want to leave you with one bit of advice, young man. Next time, ask for more. I'd have given it to you if you'd only asked for it."

His "beyond" could have gone beyond that.

And we, not coming hat-in-hand to a corporate bene-factor, but as children drawing near to our heavenly Father, need to realize who we're dealing with. Your "beyond"—the most extravagant solution to your problem, the one that would shock you if God really did it—is a piece of cake to Him, no matter how big and bold it seems to us. If we think what we're asking is beyond what He can do, we're not thinking big enough.

Because not only do His solutions transcend the natural order of things; He Himself is transcendent. Your request could never be beyond the capacity of a God who lives and originates in the realm of "beyondness."

This is how absolutely transcendent our God is. He is not just "able to do." He is "able to do [for us] *exceeding abundantly beyond.*"

And once we truly believe this astounding truth from Scripture, it changes the way we live. It changes the way we pray. It changes the way we hope. And smile. And laugh. It changes our whole outlook.

Again, His ability to go "beyond our beyond" doesn't mean He's required to take orders from us—that if we can just believe hard enough, we can force Him to agree with us about the solution we'd like to see happen. That's not at all what I'm implying. He is still sovereign. Always in ultimate control.

Being transcendent means *He* gets to decide how His "beyondness" fleshes itself out in our lives. And that should be more than okay for us—because His purposes and plans, as well as His love and grace, are so far outside the limits of where our puny minds can go, we're actually a whole lot better off just leaving the "how and when" details entirely in His hands. In fact, when we arrogantly place demands on God with our requests, we are actually doing ourselves a disservice. To limit His work to the range of our mind's capacity to plan and comprehend is to limit our own experience of the extravagant capacity of God's miracle-working potential, which spans all the way to eternity and back.

If we knew everything He was up to, we couldn't bear the weight of it. Jesus knew this when speaking with His disciples as He neared the time for His death, telling them, "I have many more things to say to you, but you cannot bear them now" (John 16:12). In reality, it is God's love and mercy, not any coldness and distance, that causes Him to keep us in a trusting relationship with Him rather than an advisory role where we snap and He jumps. He will act in our lives within the ideal time and place, always doing what is right and best. But just know that whatever He does, whenever He does it, it will be "exceeding abundantly beyond"—even if He doesn't show us everything He's doing or why He's doing it.

If we're going to enjoy His "way past" ability, we must experience it within the context of His "way past" wisdom, nature, and character.

His transcendence.

So, yes, you and I can bring any request before His throne of grace (Heb. 4:16), confident that He will hear us (1 John 5:14), confident that He will answer us (John 16:24). But before we say "amen" and thank Him for listening, we should always punctuate our prayer with one other comment: "Lord, please do this . . . *or do something better*!"

That might be the smartest thing we ever pray.

I'll take His transcendence over my intelligence any day.

Reminds me of a trip my extended family took to New York City one year—all my siblings, their spouses, their kids, my mom and dad. We were all sitting at a big, big table one night at a nice New York restaurant, and I noticed that for the second evening in a row, my brother-in-law Jessie was just nibbling on a little girlie type of appetizer. And nothing else.

You should know that Jessie, like most of the men in our family, is hardly a frou-frou appetizer kind of guy. Like my dad, my brothers, and my husband, Jessie is more the size of a big, bruising football player. If he was going to eat an appetizer, it'd be meaty and cheesy and heavy, and it would be precisely what the name suggests—nothing more than a warm-up, an appetite enhancer for the meal ahead.

So on this second night, I leaned over to him and his dainty little plate, and asked, "Jessie, you feeling okay?"

"Yeah, I'm fine. Why?"

"I've noticed you've been eating these small plates at dinner. That's not exactly from the big-boy menu," I said with a little laugh, pointing to the tiny portion in front of him.

He didn't laugh back.

Just sat there. Pained. Pitiful.

"I can't afford these fancy restaurants we've been eating in every night. I've got a family of five to feed. So I've just been getting an appetizer, then after we leave, I go out to one of the street vendors and get a big NYC hot dog."

Oh, Jessie. "Didn't you get the e-mail Dad and Mom sent before we left?"

"Huh?"

"They said we'd each need to be responsible for our own families through the day, but when we go out to eat at night, they're covering the bill. Their treat."

Let me just say, a man shouldn't let his mouth fall open like that while he's eating, even if he's only working on a pretty little appetizer.

"What!?!" he said—or something to that effect, gasping it out, all panicked and shocked.

He cocked his head a funny way, set his fork down, raised his hand for a waitress like we were in a corner booth at Denny's, and immediately changed his order to the biggest New York strip on the New York menu.

That man had been hungry for two days!—because he thought the most he could ask for was a four-bite appetizer. Beyond that, he thought the absolute most he could get was an open-air hot dog to make up for what he was missing.

But knowing that the meal you need and want is going to be covered by someone who has sufficient resources— and more—frees you up to request the best order, then sit back and gratefully receive it. Recognizing that the price has already been paid changes how you look at the menu and then prepares you to receive *His* order for you.

If you really believe what God has said about His unlimited ability, then guess what?—you may have prayed your last safe, undersized prayer for the rest of your life, both for yourself and for others. If you will start chewing on the imponderable nature of God's power on your behalf, you'll realize that voicing your wildest dreams to God does not tax His resources or place too high of a demand on His potential.

He is God.

And He is way, way past all that.

So scoot up to the table, smooth out your napkin, and start rubbing your hands together, because you don't know what all God has in store for you, your life, your family, your ministry, your future, your kids, your career. Just know that whatever it is, it will be "exceeding abundantly beyond" your wildest, mind-blowing expectations.

. . . .

Now to Him who is able to do **exceeding abundantly beyond** all that we ask or think, according to the power that works within us, to Him be the glory in the church and in Christ Jesus to all generations forever and ever. Amen.

. . . .

CHAPTER 5

Totality

". . . all that we ask or think . . ."

God and I have a track record going. And it stretches back many years now.

He helps me find things.

If it had happened just once or twice, maybe I could explain it away as good fortune. Coincidence. Dumb luck. And of course I suppose it could have been avoided altogether if I wasn't in such a steady habit of losing stuff.

But God knows this trait of mine and is patiently working on it in me. In the meanwhile, He understands who I am—and *where* I am in life—and so this has become one of the special ways I receive His love for me, enough that it has almost become like a standing joke between us.

My keys. My phone charger. Important papers.

He finds them for me.

One of the first times I really noticed His hand in this, it wasn't actually because of something I'd lost, but more because of something I really wanted. Or, well . . . dare I say it? . . . something I *needed*? I'd found this particular pair of shoes that had become my favorite ones to wear. (Don't roll your eyes now. Just hear me out.) Ministry keeps me on my feet for at least an hour or more for every session I'm teaching. And I might speak several times in one day. So it's a long time to be standing. And unlike any dress shoes I'd owned before, this particular pair gave me the ideal mix of real cute with *r-e-a-l* comfort, and I just fell in love with them.

But obviously this one pair didn't go with every outfit. And so I embarked on a mission to locate another pair in black, hoping to double the combinations of clothing ensembles I could match with these comfortable shoes.

So I went back to the store where I'd bought them, thinking "this'll be easy." But they didn't carry them anymore. Completely sold out. I asked around. I was willing to special order. I looked on eBay. I looked everywhere. But they were nowhere. Couldn't find them—not in black, not in my size. Other colors? Other sizes? Yes. What I needed? No.

Shouldn't have been that hard to locate. But oddly enough, they were. And so every few weeks, when it crossed my mind, I'd search for them online, just in case they might appear.

I *wanted* those shoes. I *needed* them to help me do what I do. And at some point in my search, when I'd just about given up, I did something I hadn't considered while I'd been rushing from store to store and from website to website.

I stopped. And prayed.

Umm . . . about shoes.

I surely did. Asked God if He'd help me find a pair of them. In black. In my size.

Yes, I know. Seemed a bit trite and ridiculous to me too at the time. That is, until a couple of days later when I typed the same search criteria I'd been using for weeks into Google, and up popped *the* shoes in *the* right size and *the* right color on a website I'd visited a dozen times before.

Remarkable.

Okay, that's nice, Priscilla. You and your shoes. Cry me a river.

But I'm telling you (quit laughing now), this experience unlocked something in my relationship with God. And I began to notice this pattern—how I'd misplace things, and look for them, and look for them, and look for them, and finally in my bewildered desperation, I would pray for God to help me.

And there it would be.

Boom.

It's like I said: track record. I'm pretty sure the Dallas CSI unit could have dusted for His fingerprints and found them all over it.

And over time, He has confirmed every suspicion.

There came a period when I was dealing with a particularly maddening loss: a missing keepsake book where for years I'd been housing a bunch of photos from my children's first months of life. This was before the days when you could store a lot of pictures on your phone. So these were real photographs—irreplaceable images I had lost. That album was so special to me, and I was in and out of it quite often. I kept it in my purse, adding stuff, jotting down memories, whipping it out at a moment's notice, holding unsuspecting strangers hostage to my family photos for far longer than they wanted, I'm sure.

Somewhere, somehow, I had lost that thing.

The season of life surrounding that time had been crazy busy. A lot of activity, a lot of traveling. That book could have been anywhere. From Florida to California to some greasy trash compactor somewhere in between— ooh, I hated the thought of it.

These were priceless memories—enough that I took the off-chance of calling every airline I'd flown, asking if they would search their lost-and-found for me. I called the hotels I'd stayed in. I called the churches and conference centers where I'd been. It was nowhere to be found.

I was crushed. I'd mentioned my upset to Jerry, but he had no idea how much I was suffering inside, or how often I racked my brain for some dim memory of where I'd seen that book last, agonizing over how I could have been so careless with something so precious. *Mmmh!*

I'm sure you've had the feeling. You look through the same closets you've already torn out twice before. You run your fingers along the same stacks and piles where you know it can't be, but maybe you overlooked it last time (although you know you couldn't, but . . .)—maybe it'll jog a new lead in your mind you haven't thought of yet.

You've looked everywhere. It *can't* be in this house, or you'd have found it by now. But still, you keep looking. "Please, God, where *is* it?"

And I had finally resorted to that approach—to prayer—after weeks and weeks of heavy lifting and a heavy heart. It was a quiet morning, months into my search for the missing book, and I was sitting down for a few moments of Bible reading when the Lord drew my eyes to a passage from Job, where this suffering saint of old had said of God, "He looks to the ends of the earth and sees *everything* under the heavens" (Job 28:24).

My heart skipped a beat.

Of course! Why should it surprise me that my heavenly Father, who "counts the number of the stars" and "gives names to all of them" (Ps. 147:4)—also owns the GPS coordinates to "everything under the heavens"? *Everything.* Even things that might be completely insignificant to someone else but mean a whole lot to me. Even things lost because of my own mistake. He knows where *everything* is located—even my boys' little keepsake book. *And since you know where it is, Lord, would You be willing to show me?*

That was my prayer.

That morning.

What I'm about to tell you is the absolute truth. I have witnesses. They'll back me up. I went to the grocery store around 10 a.m., then came back home and put everything away in the refrigerator and pantry. Then I walked back into our bedroom to take off my shoes and relax.

And . . . there it was.

That missing book—the one I'd thought, for all I knew, might have been left lying at Gate 31B in the Sydney, Australia, airport—that book with my little boys' pictures and memories in it was sitting on my pillow.

Sitting. On. My. Pillow.

Like a little gift straight from glory.

I don't exactly remember if a golden spotlight was resting on it, with little sparkles of dust twinkling in the glow. That part was probably just in my mind. But the physical book itself . . . there it was! Even the bed was made! (See, this was a genuine miracle.)

As I said, Jerry didn't completely know all the ways I'd been round and round looking for that book. He didn't know—couldn't have known—that I had just prayed and asked the Lord to help me find it a few hours earlier. But after I'd gone to the store, Jerry was moving a big piece of furniture to retrieve something that had fallen underneath, and he saw my book, picked it up, and flipped it casually on the bed.

Not knowing it was a gift from God.

I must say, with the track record the Lord had already been building up with me over the years, I don't know why I'd taken so long before going to Him and asking for His help. All I know is this: from that moment on, from then until this day, I don't waste time anymore feeling like my little problem might be too insignificant to bring to God's attention. I don't start searching underneath the sofa cushions, down on my hands and knees, without going to God directly and immediately for His sleuthing services. It's really become fairly laughable now. I ask "Where?" and He says, "Over there." Not always but often.

Saves me a ton of time.

What I'm saying is—and you will find this to be true, if you haven't already—God knows about the little things. *Your* little things. Because when they concern *you,* they're not little things anymore. The things that trouble you, no matter how unimportant or trivial they might be to your spouse, children, friends, or parents, are important to God.

For me, one way He's proven this promise is by becoming my trusty detective for missing items, even for those perfect little quotes I remember reading somewhere, sometime—*Where was it, Lord? I could really use that in this message I'm preparing. It would be so perfect in helping me make my point to the audience.* For you, His personalized ministry may take another shape entirely, but the principle is still the same: He cares about the big things, the small things, and everything in between.

Everything.

Totally.

All the Way

"Now . . .

"unto Him . . .

"who is able to do . . .

"exceeding abundantly beyond . . .

"*. . . all . . .* "

Boy, I love that word. All. In fact, I took time to research it carefully in the original language of Scripture, trying to dredge up any more depths of meaning I could learn from it. I wanted to wrap my head around exactly what was in Paul's mind when he penned his thoughts this way. And I discovered a wide consensus of scholarly opinion that says the best meaning of the word we translate as "all" in our Bibles is . . .

All.

"All" means *all.*

God is able to do . . . it all.

His activity is not confined to the spectacular and wow-worthy. Not everything He does makes headlines or invites peals of applause from the listening audience. Some of His work—dare I say, some of His *best* work—is performed on the most ordinary days, in the most ordinary places, with just ordinary people. Like us.

In other words, sometimes our problem is not that we won't believe Him for the supernatural and amazing, but that we don't believe He cares about the routine and everyday. A God-box is still a God-box, no matter where you position it in your faith. Limiting our view of God's interest and activity to the stupendous is not really much different from limiting our view of God to the boring. He doesn't exist only in the stratosphere of extravagant need. His ability comes all the way down to the ground. Where you are. Every day.

It shows up in our Wednesdays. And our laundry rooms. And our lunch plans. And our business meetings. He can alter our traffic patterns, anticipate a computer crash, help us choose the most reliable repairman from the yellow pages, and remind us we need to pick up a gallon of milk on our way home this afternoon.

By no means am I trying to minimize God to a trivial fraction of who He is. I'm only attempting to magnify the detailed and caring nature of His character. The same God who made elephants and buffaloes also made pansies and ladybugs. Big and small, He cares about them all. The miracle of how He heals a paper cut is no less God-like than the way He heals the stuff they make feature stories about on Christian television. He knows when His children are in agony, and He knows when it's just been a long day. Nothing escapes His attention.

He can do it all.

He counts the hairs on your head, the Bible says (Matt. 10:30). The one you brushed off your sweater this morning as you were getting dressed? It had a number. Just like the one that's growing in to take its place.

The dead bird you noticed at the edge of the street when you pulled out of the driveway the other morning? God was there when it fell (Matt. 10:29). Whatever tiny life it carried within itself was not too small to avoid His notice.

Why would God mention things like these in Scripture? Think what else Jesus could have been spending His time talking about—enormous plans, world-changing events, kingdom agenda items. Why would He dwell even for a moment on these unusually tender qualities about Himself? He wasn't trying to appeal to women voters. Or just show His love for animals. Or to soften His hard, Old Testament reputation. I think mainly He was simply counteracting a lie we find so easy to believe: that He may have been loving enough to die for us—taking care of our *biggest* thing—but that He's not really interested in our little things. Our daily things. Our too-small-to-mention things.

"He who did not spare His own Son, but delivered Him over for us all, how will He not also with Him freely give us all things?" (Rom. 8:32).

All things.

There is a *totality* to God's ability. It takes in *all* that concerns us. "He forgives *all* your sin; He heals *all* your diseases" (Ps. 103:3). He invites "*all* who are weary and heavy-laden" to come and experience His refreshing rest (Matt. 11:28). He says His lovingkindness "will follow me *all* the days of my life" (Ps. 23:6), which leaves me totally justified in trusting Him with *all* my heart, acknowledging Him in *all* my ways (Prov. 3:5–6), knowing that He is causing "*all* things to work together for good," for *all* the children He calls His own (Rom. 8:28). When you "seek first His kingdom and His righteousness," God promises that "*all* these things will be added to you" (Matt. 6:33)— full provision, food and clothing, love and shelter, every need.

All of it.

He is able.

So here's my question for you: Is there anything you are not vocalizing to God in prayer because you think it's too insignificant to bring up? Is there any issue you feel would be too big a waste of His time to request?

There is no minimum requirement to what He's willing to care for in our lives. He's not like Sam's Club, where they make you commit to big, bulk items before they'll let you exit the store. With God, there's no distinction. It's all the same level before this glorious One who made you and knows you and loved you enough to die for you. As hymn writer Charles Wesley put it, His is "love divine, *all* love excelling . . . Jesus, Thou art *all* compassion."

So don't think the concerns that pop up in today's nitty-gritty are meant for you to bear alone, off grid, as if they're somehow exempt from His spiritual protection, not covered under your fire insurance policy. The same God who is saving you from hell is also willing and able to save what's left of your nerves and your workweek.

Even in the fine print, God's all means all.

Totally.

If It's Not Too Much to Ask

Among the boxes we tend to build for God—the various extents to which we believe or predict He will act—is the box that confines Him to responding to us the same way others do. We often limit our expectations of Him to what we've experienced within our human interaction. We've learned, for example, that not everybody who says we should get together for lunch sometime has the slightest intention of putting it on their calendar. Not everybody who says they'll be praying for us will remember to do it. Some people hope we never find out whether or not they meant it when they told us, "If there's anything I can do, just ask."

We think God is like that too.

But as the Bible says, "God is not a man, that He should lie" (Num. 23:19). When He tells us to ask—as He does on multiple occasions in Scripture—He's not just trying to sound neighborly. He's trying to involve us in His blessing. He's wanting us to experience the fullness of our inheritance in Christ. He's using a prayer transaction to build trust and relationship.

Now let me be clear: I'm not suggesting we need to seek God's will about what we should wear before we can get dressed in the morning or decide what to pack in our kid's lunchbox. I'm saying that when we have a *concern*, when something is causing us apprehension or uneasiness, we should never shy away from bringing it to our heavenly Father just because we feel He doesn't have time for something so minor. He's invited us to do that. And His desire for relationship with us is, at least in part, why I think He's done it.

If I were to find a five-dollar bill under the passenger seat while I was cleaning out the car one day, I might feel happy enough about it to just go turn it into a latte without a thought as to where that money came from. But if I ask my husband for five dollars, I appreciate when he gives it to me. I say "thank you." I experience the tangible proof of his love for me and his desire to care for me, and I'd recognize beyond a doubt that the money came from him, not from some happenstance.

(And I *still* might get a latte.)

Asking of God doesn't make us pushy, not according to the Bible. Nor, of course, does it mean He'll give us whatever we want. But when we take Him up on His invitation to ask for what we need—both the big things and the small things—one of the greatest things He gives us is the opportunity to recognize exactly where our help is coming from. When we request and He answers, we are enabled to know beyond any doubt that He was the One working in our experience.

(By the way, this is a great gift to your children as well. Lead them to pray about a problem at school or in one of their friendships, and let them see and feel what it's like to watch God respond.)

When we truly ask of the Lord, we're not just hoping in general; we're relating with our Father. We're asking and seeking and knocking, just as His Word instructs us to do (Matt. 7:7). And when He gives, when we find, when the door is opened to us, we don't sit there wondering how in the world *that* happened. By inviting us to ask, He is continually connecting His life with ours. Every blessing becomes another noticeable expression of His loving care, even if it's no more than finding the flashlight batteries or a button that fell off our sleeve.

He is able to do "all that we ask." *Beyond* it, actually.

But even *that's* not all. (And this part gets me so excited, I can barely stand it.) Since we can't often pinpoint the exact reason for the ache in our heart that needs healing or the worry that's keeping us from sleeping, God doesn't need to wait for us to find the right words before He responds. He is willing to do beyond what we ask, yes, but He'll even do beyond what we can "think."

Man, this keeps getting bigger all the time.

The extent of information that I could transpose into a prayer request is pretty vast. If given enough time and journaling space, I could ask for a million things or more—about myself, about my heart, about my marriage, about my kids, about our ministry, about our future, about our church, about my friends, about our city, about our nation, about Haiti, about Africa, about almost anything.

You know what I mean because I bet you could do it too.

The gigabytes of data that could live within the phrase "all that we ask" would probably blow out every circuit breaker in the neighborhood.

But what about the things that are beyond what we can even find the right words to ask for? Because, for example, we can't know the future. We can't fully grasp the depths of hurt and pain in the world . . . or even in our own hearts. We can't truly know another's intentions or even our own at times (usually *most* of the time).

Not to worry. The things we don't know how to pray, as well as the things we don't even know to be praying for at all, are still under His control. He can do all that we can "ask *or* think."

More than we can imagine.

Did you hear that? The vast extent to which your mind could draw together what, in your estimation, would be the most exquisite plan for the solution you need doesn't even begin to touch the hem of His ability. He does *beyond* it.

Beyond all your words.

Beyond all your thoughts.

So in His love, He makes allowances for these limitations and weaknesses of ours. In those times when "we do not know how to pray as we should . . ."

> . . . the Spirit Himself intercedes for us with groanings too deep for words; and He who searches the hearts knows what the mind of the Spirit is, because He intercedes for the saints according to the will of God. (Rom. 8:26–27)

Beyond what we could think to ask are things that only God knows. And out there, in here, wherever our words come up short, His Spirit fills in the blanks, not allowing anything to touch our lives that cannot be co-opted to conform to His will.

You and I are completely covered.

Totally.

Because God is able.

. . . .

Now to Him who is able to do exceeding abundantly beyond **all that we ask or think,** according to the power that works within us, to Him be the glory in the church and in Christ Jesus to all generations forever and ever. Amen.

. . . .

CHAPTER 6

Turbo

". . . according to the power that works within us . . ."

Have you ever gotten stuck behind a slow car in traffic—hemmed inside the right lane while others pass you in such a steady stream on the left that you can't pull over and join them? The only thing worse, I suppose, is being stuck on a long, winding, country road like the ones near our house in rural Texas, where there's no left-lane escape at all.

As long as the culprit is a farmer's old rusty pickup or tractor, you at least know the reason for the slowdown. But recently when I was bottled up in a situation like that, the car that was going twenty miles under the speed limit wasn't a golf cart or a riding lawn mower. It was a late-model, powder blue, Ford Mustang GT.

Now I don't pretend to know a lot about cars. But come on, even a girl like me, who'd rather talk about vintage home décor than vintage cars (well, *any* cars actually) knows a few things about Mustangs. They're high-performance, they're V8 engines, they're big-time horsepower . . . and they don't jam up the road by failing to maintain proper speed. Mustangs are usually the ones forcing *you* to move over, revving up close behind you, riding your tail, growling at you like they own the road.

But not this one. Not this day. This person was obviously in no rush to get wherever he was going.

And I was behind him.

On a two-lane road.

Stuck.

I'd like to say I was perfectly patient and easygoing, whistling the tune of a hymn while following said Mustang. It'd make me feel so godly to tell you how I took advantage of the extra time to strengthen my prayer life or to quote Scripture. But I ain't gonna do that, 'cause I'd be lying.

Finally, after what seemed like an eternity, the horizon leveled out and I saw that the path was clear enough to take a chance at jumping into the other lane to pass the very non-tractor, non-country-like Mustang. As I steered toward the left and accelerated, gunning the mighty

Shirer-mobile past this fancy but slow-going sports car, I couldn't keep from darting a quick, irritated glance at its driver. (Don't tell me you wouldn't have done the same thing.)

And, whoa!—not what I was expecting. Not the kind of car owner I anticipated seeing behind the wheel. This was not a teenager doing more texting than driving, or a cool, carefree yuppie with tinted sunglasses and the wind blowing through his hair. The driver of *this* Mustang was a little old grandma-looking woman with gray hair and slumped shoulders that barely made it over the steering wheel.

I wish you could've seen it. It was comical.

But in one way, it was sweet and endearing. Softened the situation a bit for me. And as I zoomed ahead quickly to pass her and then trade places for first in line, I pondered this mismatched image between old woman and sports car and found it to be somewhat spiritually enlightening.

Think of all the power that lived under the hood of that Mustang. Think of all that automotive engineering going to waste. A car like hers, equipped with so much explosive thrust and muscle—I mean, it was practically capable of running a NASCAR race. So you'd think she could at least get it up over thirty miles an hour, right? And yet there she was, just puttering along, leaving all that harnessed power untapped, untried, untested. I wondered if this precious woman was even aware that all those horses were under the hood, just waiting for the opportunity to maximize their potential.

So as I glanced back at her, fading farther and farther behind me, I didn't just see a little old lady in a blue Mustang. I saw . . . maybe me. Maybe you. Endowed by God with an enormous amount of power, yet tinkering along at a spiritual snail's pace, taking up a lane but not really letting Him take us anywhere. Trading adventure for what feels to us (deceptively) like complete control. As a result, not only do we miss out on feeling the wind of destiny and abundance in our *own* hair, we also potentially clog up the pipeline of blessing for others coming up behind us. We forfeit opportunities to show our children and those we disciple what happens when His foot is on the accelerator of our lives.

We were created to *floor* people when they see God's mighty power at work inside us. Our juiced-up spiritual engines were made to purr with the joy and strength He provides. We were meant to wheel into each day's traffic with His high-octane ability and supernatural power coursing through our fuel lines.

We've got power. And by recognizing how much we're actually sitting on and operating it at full capacity, we locate the keys to experiencing what Ephesians 3:20–21 is offering us.

Inside Job

Power.

You've got it.

If you're a believer in Christ, you've had it all along.

The moment you believed (Eph. 1:13), you received the Holy Spirit. Did you hear that? The *Spirit of Almighty God*—complete with enough horsepower to carry you victoriously all the way to eternity—dwells inside you and me right now as believers in Christ. Please don't ever skim over that statement casually, even though you may have heard it a million times before. God Himself has supernaturally taken up residence on the inside of us—all His greatness, all His grandeur, all His fullness, all His ability . . .

All His power.

In you. In me.

Right now.

What a travesty it would be to let it—to let Him—just sit there. Untapped and unused. Barely if ever igniting His power, afraid to punch it, to see what it can do. Have we decided our faith is better off just playing it safe on the spiritual back roads, in the slow lane, hardly letting it drive us anywhere other than to church on Sunday?

Power.

That's what we have.

Power.

I've thought a lot about you as I've written this chapter. I've wondered if the circumstances you may be facing right now have caused you to feel a bit powerless. I only wonder because I know how powerless *I've* felt on some days— like my eight-year-old son feels when he wrestles with his dad. It's a good match for about five minutes, but after a while he's just exhausted and lies there in a heap under his father's big, bulky chest, unable to move or fight back. Life can do that to you. Can make you feel kaput, done, finished, over it. But I know from the testimony of God's Word that "power" is one thing we should never feel short on. Even if we do get tired, exhausted even, we don't need to feel impotent. God's power doesn't negate weariness; it just enables us to press through it with an uncommon persistence. No matter how tall our challenges are, His power in us is greater still.

Paul said the power of God that whirls and throbs within us is a power of "surpassing greatness" (Eph. 1:19). It is "immeasurable" (HCSB), "incomparably great" (NIV), "incredible" (NLT), a matter of "utter extravagance" (MSG).

Paul, in fact, declared that his whole ministry as an apostle was initiated by, established on, and animated through the "working of [God's] power" (Eph. 3:7). And, hey, Paul's was the kind of ministry that wouldn't even let a stretch in prison knock him off stride.

We're talking about more power than we can imagine.

God the Father reached down from heaven and raised His Son *from the dead* with this power. Think about the amount of energy and coercion it takes just to get your teenager out of bed in the morning. Try wrapping your head around how much power it would take to rouse the bloodied, beaten, buried corpse of a man who'd been shrouded in death for three days! To give Him new life in a new body! If you could somehow put that kind of power on a measuring scale, if you could tape together enough forests of yardsticks to lay beside it from end to impossible end, *then* you'd be looking at the power that's inside you right now, wherever you are, whatever you're dealing with (Eph. 1:19–20).

It's not just *your* power. It's *His*.

Remember in chapter 3 of this book when we talked about the *Truth* of this statement: "He is able to do"? If you recall, I told you that Paul's word choice in describing God's ability and power was the Greek word *dunamai*. Well, here's something else to consider along that vein: the way Paul used the word in reference to our God denotes a power that is inherent to its owner. In other words, Paul wanted us to know that power is not just a tool that's in God's hand; power is part of God's very nature and character. It's intrinsic, woven into the fabric of His essence. God doesn't *have* power; He is power. He is the *all-powerful One*. Power is built right into His personhood, so it exists in unending supply.

This means the vast ocean of His power has no bounds. It knows no limits. And it is from this unending, boundless, limitless supply of God's power-engrained character that we (yes, you and I) draw our own power. We are empowered "according to" this same deep, rich storehouse of strength. The power He gives us is in proportion with the full, unlimited measure of *His* divine power. The power inside us is a reflection of—it's in keeping with—all the power He possesses.

You get it *all*.

Just like I do.

And—I'm sorry, but I can't help but digress for just a moment, because this point makes me think of something that might bring you a large measure of freedom before you even finish this chapter.

When you see Him at work in somebody else's life or hear a testimony of how He's performed a miraculous deliverance, healing, or restoration for another person—there is never a need to become discouraged or envious of His activity on their behalf. Since God's power is intrinsic to His character, it can never decrease or be depleted. His ability displayed in the life of another is not draining away the likelihood that He'll have enough power left over to handle your situation too.

The power of God is not a zero-sum game, where whatever good He expends on one person or situation is depleted from you and others. The reason we can freely "rejoice with those who rejoice" (Rom. 12:15)—without jealousy, discouragement, or (come on, admit it) secret pain or anger or sadness—is because God is no less powerful now than He was before He did what He did for that other person. He is all-power, all the time.

Never-ending.

Continuous.

Endless.

Eternal.

All that and a bag of chips.

This unrelenting supply of power is the bottomless well from which we draw.

Now it is possible, of course, to have all this power and it not be "working." (Think about the woman in the Mustang.) Why else would Paul specify "the power that *works* within us?" The Holy Spirit's power can be in you, ready to be activated and utilized, yet remain dormant and largely untapped.

It's similar to how you could bring home one of those amazing Nespresso coffeemakers (which I will neither confirm nor deny that I am completely in love with)—and then never plug it in. The device is fully capable of performing a whole bunch of cool, coffee-making functions. Lush flavors are sitting there just waiting to be enjoyed. But if you never turn it on or plug it in, it won't make any kind of foamy, hot, goodness-in-a-cup no matter *which* button you push. It won't work until you put the power to work.

You could stand in the shower all afternoon, right there under the spigot, hoping to be clean and refreshed, but you'd walk away in the same smelly condition as before if you never turned on the water (which I know firsthand is possible, because I'm a mother of three sons).

You could admire the cozy look and clean surfaces of your gas fireplace, but it'll never warm up the room on a cold night unless you fire up the jets. Your local utility company could be faithfully flowing electrical current into your home, but unless you flip the light switch inside your bedroom, you'll still be in the dark, operating in primitive candlelight, no matter how many kilowatt hours are available to you.

Power.

Power that's not working.

It's possible.

Yes, we can have God's power inside and not use it—not put it to work. Even though *He* has the ability to do "exceeding abundantly beyond all that we ask or think," we have the ability to let all *His* ability lie dormant in our lives by not flipping the switch.

That's the key—flipping the switch—activating the power of God within us.

So how do we do it?

We do it by responding in obedience to the voice of God, yielding to the conviction of His Spirit, and operating under His leading in our lives. The more we "walk by the Spirit" (Gal. 5:16–25), refusing to gratify and yield to the flesh, His power and influence continues to grow and mature in us. As a result, we see more and more of the Spirit's power start to "work" in our lives. Soon we're noticing the fruit of the Spirit springing up from our life and the gifts of His Spirit edifying His body through us.

And then—oh, then!—in response to and in conjunction with the power operating in our lives, we will begin to see the "exceeding abundantly beyond" activity of God.

The more of God's power we flip the switch for and the more operational it becomes, the more we will experience God's work in our circumstances. One is a prerequisite for the next.

Fill 'er Up

Here's what I'm afraid of. Here's what I want to be sure doesn't keep happening to you or to me.

I think we're sometimes in the habit of seeing only thimblefuls of God's activity occurring in our lives—and considering that to be normal. We think small things are all that God is capable of doing because that's all we've ever seen Him do. So we walk down to the shoreline of His ability, carrying our little cups and containers, dipping our little thimbles of expectation into the ocean of His vast greatness. We think that's all we can expect, so that's all we bring. Then we're disappointed and discouraged when we experience only a thimble's worth of God's activity in our circumstances. That's usually when we accuse and blame Him: *God, You must not really be able. God, You must not really be good.* But honestly, we got exactly what we came expecting. He doesn't give us more than the capacity we bring Him will allow.

Bring a thimble?

Fill a thimble.

But if we would come to the ocean of God's measure-less power bringing our wheelbarrows and five-gallon buckets, that's exactly how much of Him we'd get to experience.

Bring a bucket? Fill a bucket.

Bring a wheelbarrow? Fill a wheelbarrow.

Bring a two-ton tanker? Fill a two-ton tanker.

The volume you bring is the volume you'll receive. What will that measure be for you? The more of God's power operating in your life, the bigger your capacity and opportunity to experience Him.

Recently the Lord has allowed me to hear about some stunning, epic, jaw-dropping miracles He has performed in the lives of others. I'm not talking about stories I've read in books or heard through the grapevine. I mean real, twenty-first-century people I've actually talked with, peo-ple who have told me firsthand testimonies that made the hair on the back of my neck stand straight up. Their expe-rience with God was grand and amazing. Awe-inspiring.

Two-ton tanker-sized miracles.

And with each of these individuals, I've noticed a com-mon thread. They depend heavily and consistently on the Spirit of God. They've followed Him faithfully to extreme lengths of obedience. And they've been willing to put themselves in risky places of faith at God's bidding. With these kinds of switches flipped—these kinds of "containers" making room for His ability—they have found themselves in prime positions to experience a larger measure of God's activity.

God wants us backing up our trucks to the ocean and renting some heavy hauling equipment. Better yet, He just wants us to come down here to live—where we can cannonball ourselves into the deep end, empty ourselves of every doubt and inhibition, and live completely immersed in the power He's made available to us. The more the Spirit's power is activated in your life, the more your capacity to experience God increases. He is faithful to fill that which you bring ready to receive.

Powered Up

This all-important issue of power working within us is so much deeper and wider than we think. It truly touches all of life. It produces changes in us that are every bit as miraculous as any change in our circumstances could ever be.

If you look carefully—beyond the halfway mark of Ephesians where Paul's doxology appears—you'll see that the remaining chapters and verses in the book are all connected. The fourth chapter begins with the word "Therefore . . ."

And any time you come across the word *therefore* in the Scriptures, you ought to take a minute to see what it's *there for*.

Therefore what?

Therefore, because of God's ability operating within your heart—because of everything entailed within the chapters and verses leading up to the "God Is Able" statement of Ephesians 3:20–21—you are empowered to "walk in a manner worthy of the calling with which you have been called" (4:1). You're empowered to experience the kind of changes inside you that start changing things around you.

His power, for example, is able to inspire in you actual expressions of patience and gentleness, love and acceptance, genuine peace and contentment (4:2–5), even in those times when you've been misunderstood, ignored, or flat-out betrayed. (Or, say, for those times when you're behind a slow car in traffic.)

It can transform your reactions and responses.

His power is able to flow through the giftings He's placed within you, so that you can serve Him, serve your church, and serve your fellow believers in a way that fulfills His purposes for you and produces unity and spiritual fruit in the process—all while keeping you humbly content. And all for His glory (4:11–16).

It can transform your contribution to His body.

His power is able to shut your mouth, stifle your anger, make you scrupulously honest, help you extend true forgiveness, purify you sexually, and show you how to become the same person in private as you claim to be in public (4:25–32).

It can transform your character.

His power is able to restore your desire for your husband, to renew your love for your wife, to refashion your marriage into one that honors God, not because you've reached some level of perfection but because of the heart of grace you share with one another (5:22–33). His power can also lead you to parent your children with loving, caring responsibility, to perform your job with diligence and integrity, to treat your employees with understanding and character-driven leadership (6:1–8).

It can transform your home, your work life, your reputation, everything.

All of this is ours when we start putting the power within us to work.

When you really think about it, a lot of the things we ask Him to transform—maybe even the *It* circumstances in our lives—might just fall within the scope of one of those categories that Paul addressed in the latter half of Ephesians. Seriously. Many of the things we're asking God to change, He's already given us the key to at least begin the process of that transformation: His surpassing, incomparable, incredible power. A simple decision to recognize and utilize the power that God has already put within us would have a staggering ripple effect of implications on every area of our lives.

It's easy for us to spend most of our time treating symptoms, patching up problem areas, papering things over, getting by, asking God for solutions that His power has already given us the capability of solving. If we truly started operating in the power that He has granted us, letting Him truly scrub our thoughts and actions to a deep-down clean, I wonder how many of those external, surface issues would resolve themselves.

I'm just sayin'.

That's what the *therefore* is *there for*. Paul wanted to tell us all the things that can be transformed in our lives and all that we have the potential to become if we will put the turbo power of Ephesians 3:20–21 to work.

Therefore . . . let's start living like the powerful people we are.

Let's "be strong in the Lord and in the strength of His might" (Eph. 6:10).

This Means War

I recall one morning several years ago, standing over a saucepan in the kitchen, spatula in hand, slowly moving scrambled eggs over the burner. The scurry of little feet hustled behind me as the early morning rush ensued—clothes to put on, teeth to brush, backpacks to put in the backseat. In the meanwhile, I was in charge of filling tummies: breakfast for now and a packed lunch for later.

Soon, two little boys sat in stools behind me at the kitchen nook waiting for their breakfasts, the baby still asleep in his crib. I spooned eggs, bacon, and a slice of cinnamon toast onto a plate, set it down in front of one child, then returned to the stove to prepare the next.

And it was only a few moments later—seconds really, hardly enough time for him to swallow more than a bite or two—before he lobbed out a fifty-pound question that landed with a noticeable thud at my back.

"Mom . . . will I ever be in a war?"

Excuse me? You know how it is with kids and questions. You learn never to be surprised. And yet sometimes you can't be anything else *but* surprised. Perhaps he had awakened that morning amid a wild, dream-like battle sequence, and his foggy imagination was still wrestling with the idea. Maybe he'd actually been stewing over this issue within himself for quite a while, without saying. Or maybe (I don't know), maybe a deep God-whisper had just then settled into his soul, right over his plate of scrambled eggs.

Wherever it came from . . . out it came.

My son. A soldier?

I whipped my head around just long enough to flash him a sideways grin, then a furrowed brow . . . then a nervous chuckle when I noticed his brother giving him the same blank, curious stare as mine.

"Babe, what are you talking about?" I asked, as nonchalantly as possible.

But, no, he was serious. Concerned even, as attested by his melancholy expression, fork motionless in his hand, a wad of half-eaten food still piled inside one cheek.

"You know," he said, "will I ever be in a war? Like a war with . . . with Satan?"

Wait . . . *what*? Bible study? For breakfast? I wasn't quite ready.

But he wasn't letting this go. He really wanted to know.

Like, now.

This was the same boy who regularly wore a superhero cape to the grocery store. A boy who often wielded a Star Wars lightsaber at playtime. How does a mom answer a spiritually complex question like this in a way that a child can understand—much less at seven in the morning over scrambled eggs?

So as I walked across with the other plate of breakfast in my hand, I brought a side order of prayer with me as well. The plate went to my other son; the prayer went to my Father. I could feel my heart beat a bit faster and louder, echoing in my ears. Then each beat began to drum out a settled, serious answer, and I said . . .

"Son, you're in a battle. Already. Both of you are."

And don't we know it.

And we never outgrow it.

What I said to them is what I want to say to you. Our lives are one long battle after another, waged by the same enemy who's been trying to destroy us since the moment we first passed through our mother's womb. We feel the battle in our homes, in our relationships, in our bodies, in our heads. We hear the taunts challenging our attitudes, our reactions, our impulses, our work ethic. It takes the form of arguments and silences and tears and betrayals. We sense it in everything from our serving-size portions to our television viewing habits. It's both everyday and out of the blue.

Struggles. Frustrations. Fissures. Pressures.

The battle.

The spiritual war.

Paul wants us to know that the battle my son asked about—the one you're staring at right now in your life—"is not against flesh and blood, but against the rulers, against the powers, against the world forces of this darkness, against the spiritual forces of wickedness in the heavenly places" (Eph. 6:12). Against Satan. Against fierce spiritual opposition.

And yet even with all of that assembled military might drawn up in battle formation against us, we are not outmatched . . . because we have armor: the "full armor of God" (6:11). Truth to fight the lies. Grace-given righteousness to fight the guilt and regret. Peace to fight the impatience. Faith to fight the sneak attacks of doubt. And to top it all off, salvation and His Spirit to guarantee eternal victory.

We have power.

"Really?" my little Superman said with a smile. "We've got armor? And weapons?"

"Yes, sweetie . . . and power."

And that means, with God's help, we can win the battle every single time.

. . . .

Now to Him who is able to do exceeding abundantly beyond all that we ask or think, **according to the power that works within us,** to Him be the glory in the church and in Christ Jesus to all generations forever and ever. Amen.

. . . .

CHAPTER 7

Tribute

". . . to Him be the glory . . ."

I don't know anybody who doesn't like a good two-for-one sale.

I mean, coupons are fine, sure. But for my money, no bargain can put quite the same skip in a shopper's step as the one that lets you take home a whole second item for FREE!

Zero point zero zero.

Now obviously, I know there's a sneaky marketing, markup strategy embedded in there somewhere that ends up slipping more out of my pocket than I probably realize. I understand the math is not entirely what it seems. But I choose to live in my blissful BOGO version of reality, thankful to have an extra apple juice or soup mix or Old Navy top that I can tuck away for later use. For nothing.

But that's just me.

Two for one is always good in my book.

And in *this* book, as we reach the final phrase in Paul's doxology on the "beyondness" of God's ability, I find myself marveling at how God multiplies His blessings. When He moves within our lives, He doesn't stop at doing just one miracle, at one time, in one way, for one purpose. The abundant capabilities and possibilities of God's activity position us over the bonus bin, because He does nothing without doing a whole *bunch* of things at the same time.

He is a two-for-one specialist . . . and then some.

So let me just reset things for us here. Remember our pizza? We're at the crust now. The widest part. The part that holds it all together. The part that rings around every layer of goodness and flavor and seasoning, giving us a place to grab on and fully experience what we've been discovering all this time.

I'm aware the crust may not be everybody's favorite. I mean, it's really not what most people buy their pizza for. And sometimes, it's a taste that has to grow on you. I've seen my kids, for example, scarf down the pepperoni and cheese part of the pizza, nibbling all the way up to the crispy edges, then piling up the crusts on their plates like mutton bones at a Robin Hood feast. Pizza debris. Those are the scraps we'd leave for the dog, I guess, if we *had* a dog. (Which we don't. And won't. Every time my boys beg me for one, I tell them the same thing: *I can only keep three things alive.* And they need to be thankful that they're one of them.)

No, in most situations, the crust isn't what we come for. Way too bland. We want the meaty part, the "beyond, beyond" part. The part oozing with signs of His abundant ability working in our circumstances. We want to be filled, to be satisfied, to feel good again. We want to be reminded that He loves us and cares for us and knows what we're up against.

And because we are His children, He does all that. Our Father takes pleasure in tending to our needs, supplying our hearts with more than ample nourishment for each day, the same way I delight in seeing my little men blessed by what I set out for them on the table.

That's the cheesy, greasy, gooey part.

But even I know that I'm not here just to feed my kids. Even I know there's more to this parenting business than the homework help and the chore charts and the coloring pages that fill our hours until bedtime every day. Jerry and I realize, even while we're actively engaging with our boys in these necessary routines of life, we're also doing something much bigger here. Much grander. Much more long-range and long-term. It's bigger than us. It's bigger than them. It's bigger than just what's going on right now. It's big.

And when our Father shows Himself to be "beyond" able in our lives, we can be sure that He's thinking much bigger than just meeting this one need on this one day. Whenever He obliterates one of our challenges or obstacles, whenever He rearranges the whole way our hearts feel, behave, and obey in a certain situation, He's accomplishing what we've asked of Him . . . and more.

Much, much more.

Glory Be

When God drew our hearts into fellowship with Him, when He applied Christ's blood to our boatload of sinfulness, that could easily have been enough good news to last us a lifetime—rescuing us from the punishment our rebellion so rightly deserved. Saving us from everlasting destruction.

But that wasn't all He was doing. According to Ephesians 2:6–7, He has not only spared our souls from hell, He has "raised us up with Him, and seated us with Him in the heavenly places in Christ Jesus."

Seated.

With Him.

In heavenly places.

That's hardly just a get-out-of-hell card. It is an engraved invitation to the head table. This is indescribable privilege and opportunity—for people like *us*, who know what *we've* done.

But even *that's* not all. Those same verses in Ephesians 2 also tell us that God considers His rescue of us—His transfer of divine grace to our hopelessly overdrawn account—as one of His prize accomplishments. He is so proud of what He's done with us—how He's reclaimed us and saved us—that throughout all "the ages to come," He is going to be taking us around, showing us off, allowing our lives to give riveting, lasting testimony to His kindness, His power, His love, His ability.

His glory.

"To Him be the glory . . ."

That's how Paul says it.

We need a good, healthy reminder every now and then—each of us do—that life is not all about us and ours, about me and mine. Yes, God in His providence has ascribed deep value to you and to me. And yes, our lives *do* matter. Our concerns *do* affect Him. He has chosen by His great mercy to elevate us to a height of dignity and significance.

But let's be crystal clear about things—ultimately, our lives are all and completely about *Him*.

We exist today for *His* fame.

We are examples of *His* patience and long-suffering.

We bear witness to what *His* love is like and can do.

We honor *His* name with our living, breathing presence.

We're here for *Him*. We're here for *His* pleasure.

For *His* praise and *His* glory.

So when we come to Him with our needs and requests, with our aches and our longings, one of the greatest reasons why we can be so confident in Him is because—let's just say it—*God is gettin' Him some glory* when He acts on our behalf. One way or the other. You can count on that.

When He laid down the carpet of earth beneath our feet and stretched the sky overhead in all its starry brilliance, He was doing it primarily to broadcast His glory (Ps. 19:1). When He provided manna from heaven to sustain His people in the wilderness, He did it to feed them but also to amaze them with His glory (Exod. 16:7). When He sent His Son to us as a baby, it was to redeem the lost, yes, but it was also for the purpose of receiving "glory to God in the highest" (Luke 2:14). For truly, what we see in Christ, above all, is God's glory—"glory as of the only begotten from the Father, full of grace and truth" (John 1:14).

His ability in our circumstances is *personal* but also *perpetual.*

It keeps on going and giving and multiplying, paying tribute to God long after the miracle itself first occurred.

When Jesus was told the grim news of His friend Lazarus's failing health, He said to His disciples, "This sickness is not to end in death, but for the *glory of God*, so that the Son of God may be glorified by it" (John 11:4, emphasis added). And still today, everything He restores, rekindles, and resurrects in our lives is specifically designed to exhibit His power, to bring Him glory (Ps. 79:9).

Every time.

The reason He goes "exceeding abundantly beyond all that we ask or think" is not *only* because He loves us and wants to put this problem back together for us. He's also intent on receiving glory.

And when we look at life—all of it, altogether—that should be how we see it. We are a walking, talking means of glorifying God. Boil it all down to the gravy (or the crust of the pizza pie) and that's the bottom line.

Think of it this way: When we willfully sin and reject His loving shepherding over our lives, the greatest costs to us are not the consequences we suffer, but the everyday instances when we could have been giving Him glory and didn't. What we risk by our feeble, forgetful prayerlessness—more than anything—is the opportunity to actively participate in what He is doing for our good *and His glory*.

Somehow, we think that by not allowing ourselves to over-believe or over-expect, we're giving ourselves a fallback. We think we're helping God out by not forcing Him into a corner where, if He doesn't respond, we might make Him look bad. We're guarding our hearts and our watching friends or children from disappointment, from discouragement, from thinking of God as uncaring and unmoved. No, what we're doing is selling short His glory for pennies on the dollar.

But when our eyes look through our prayer requests and see not only a chance for personal relief but also an opening for God to burst forth in well-deserved glory, we're speaking the language of His heart. We're letting this problem or issue do what God wanted it to accomplish all along when He allowed it into our lives—to showcase His ability, to spotlight His strength, to invite the healing showers of His sustained glory.

God is not inclined to act with power and magnificence toward us if there's not any glory in it for Him (James 4:3). But just imagine—little old us and our little old needs—being commissioned by Almighty God for the purpose of giving tribute to His power. That's strong. It changes the whole color scheme. This problem that used to clash with everything, stick out like a sore thumb—it was all you could see. But when you turn your head a certain way now and change your perspective a bit, while it's still very noticeable, it looks like it might hold some promise here.

It's a glory maker, not just a troublemaker.

If that's not how you've been seeing things lately, I understand that. You're not the only one. All of us, if we're being real honest, have done more feeling sorry for ourselves than feeling privileged at being broken vessels for God's use and glory.

But today's a new day—a chance to start all over again, knowing He is still able to work with our failures and faithlessness, with our weakness and need. In fact, He loves doing that. It's just another day in the getting-glory office for Him. Every time He leads us to a place of total surrender, with everything offered up to Him for His use, what we're really seeing is the work of God, because He alone is able to make that kind of change in this kind of heart. He alone can turn our kind of problems into the most incredible kind of worship.

And I only know one thing to say about that.

To Him be the glory.

When Glory Goes to Church

A few years ago, some billionaire here in town built a big, honkin' new home for his football team. Cowboys Stadium is a gleaming, silver edifice to Dallas Cowboy glory and to the man who dreamed it up, smack in the middle of a depressed economy.

I remember vividly the year it opened because it played host to the Super Bowl—which is supposed to be a festive, party-driven, resort-type experience for the fans and media who attend. Think Miami. Think New Orleans. Think Pasadena, California. The time when it was here, however, people had to think about packing their long johns, because a freak winter storm landed in Dallas the last week of January and wouldn't pull up for days, nearly right up to kickoff.

But even on that cold day, just like on most Sundays ever since in the fall and winter, more than 80,000 fans converged on that facility to tailgate and trash-talk and take in the spectacle of NFL football. Happens all the time. If the event is big enough, they'll put in temporary seats to accommodate ten or fifteen thousand more. They'll even sell tickets so people can watch on video screens in the concourses—or even *outside*, just to be near the stadium while the game is going on.

When the glory of that place is on full display, folks come from all over to see it.

Imagine, though, if it wasn't that way. What would happen if after all that work and investment, after all that expense and extravagance by the owner, nobody came around to watch what was going on? Nobody advertised it or printed up tickets. Everybody stayed home and found other things to do. The teams came, the coaches came, the referees came, they played the game, but nobody saw it. Nobody recognized the enormity of what was taking place there.

Crazy.

So why should we be surprised that when God works, He wants an audience? When God works in you, He wants others to know about it. When He works in them, He wants you to know about it.

And so He takes us to church. Within the family and fellowship of your local congregation, as well as the larger church in general (God's people united in Christ across all cultures and countries and communities of faith), He has established an audience for His ability. When His miraculous, need-meeting activity occurs in our lives, He intends to use it as faith-building evidence of His power among those who hear us tell it and see us changed by it.

"To Him be the glory," the Bible says, *"in the church
. . ."*

Among the many magnets that draw people to Christ
are the manifold testimonies of His work in the lives of
His people. His glory is meant to be shown, not just to
ourselves in our own living rooms, not just for our own
benefit and personal amazement, but for church-wide
display. Just think: if He receives glory from us *individually* by showing Himself strong in our lives, what kind of
glory must He receive when it's rising up to Him from
tens, dozens, hundreds, perhaps thousands of others, all
at one time?

That's the kind of tribute He expects and deserves
from His investment in us. That's the kind of glory that
rumbles like thunder in our hearts when we're around it,
when people are telling it and living it. We don't just hear
it in our own earbuds. We feel it thumping in our feet and
tingling through our whole bodies. We experience it in the
context of shared friendship, not merely alone in our car
with the windows rolled up.

And remember, the threshold for what qualifies
as God-activity in our lives—the kind that's worthy
of church celebration and coffee conversation—is not
restricted to movie-length miracles. Every single example
of His grace and mercy and kindness and endurance is

worthy of acclaim. To tell your friends. To tell your Bible study group. To tell your neighbors and coworkers and workout companions.

We, as blood-bought members of His family, can talk up His ability anywhere we go and expect Him to attract notice in the direction of His glory.

In the church.

The phone rang at a pastor's home one night after he'd gone to bed. Emergency: the church building was on fire. So he leapt into his clothes, sped over to the scene, and sure enough the entire structure was engulfed in flames, firefighters already suited up and in action. People in the neighborhood, hearing the sirens and the rush of activity, had come out of their homes to watch the drama for themselves from nearby streets and front yards. And the longer the blaze intensified, as more people began hearing about it and showing up with shocked, heavy hearts to watch it, the whole area swelled with onlookers.

Someone standing near the pastor, looking around at the gathered crowd, said rather introspectively, "You know, I don't think there's ever been this many people at church before."

The pastor, still gazing straight ahead, could only come up with one answer: "Yeah, well, this church has never been on fire before."

When we become a gathered group of testifying brothers and sisters—truly praying, truly believing, truly supporting each other, truly rejoicing—the world around us won't be able to keep from hearing about it and gathering around to see it.

And God in heaven will bask in the glory, then draw all men unto Himself.

Now and Forever

"To Him be the glory . . ."

". . . in the church . . ."

". . . in Christ Jesus . . ."

And what's more, the tribute goes on "to all generations forever and ever."

Paul finally places a period on the tail end of this glorious, run-on sentence—but not before stretching out the extent of its glory to the far horizons. Beyond ourselves. Beyond our problems and needs and hurts and desires. Even beyond our lifetimes.

Forever.

And ever.

I'm sure you've probably brought your latest request before the Father at sometime throughout this day, perhaps at multiple times. Maybe early this morning. Maybe while driving here and there from work or between your various stops and appointments. Maybe it was late in the evening when you laid your most recent prayer on His doorstep under the quiet weight of darkness, before what has turned into another long night of concern and heartache. I don't know.

But I do know that when you and I approach God for help, filled with our cares and distresses, our prayers are not confined to this calendar date, to this particular month and year. What may seem to be His silence and avoidance from where you sit today is already reverberating in future places. If not right here, if not right now, you can be sure His ability is taking visible, tangible shape somewhere, even if beyond the scope of your current sightline.

You and I are living right this minute on a tiny dot of time within a vast sea of God-moments. And the ripple effect of today's prayer, today's faith—today's *now*—spirals out in all directions for all eternity, bumping something here, affecting something there, all under God's watchful eye and wisdom. Each time we turn to Him, each time we trust, each time we bring our all to the surpassing greatness of *His* all, we find ourselves instantly connected to every future time zone where His ability lives. We link up across generations where He is already working, present-tense, to make His glory known.

When you think back, that's where these two verses have been taking us all along—from this current pinprick of time we call today (our "now") with all its pressing needs and battles, into the majestic expanse of His ability that flows out to the unseen edges of eternity. That's the power He is able to funnel not only into our everyday lives, but into our futures, into our children and grandchildren, into our churches, into our nations, into every moment His presence fills.

What a miracle that we can trust in God's ability, that we can sit or stand in this place and be part of what He's doing all over the place, that we can stretch out our faith, and even our need, and give Him the honor, the glory—the tribute—He deserves.

Forever and ever.

To all generations.

Amen.

. . . .

Now to Him who is able to do exceeding abundantly beyond all that we ask or think, according to the power that works within us, **to Him be the glory in the church and in Christ Jesus to all generations forever and ever. Amen.**

. . . .

FINALLY

Tell It

Hey, we made it.

It always feels good to finish a book, whether you're writing one or reading one. And I hope this one has been a welcome, refreshing, encouraging place for you to spend some time.

I've loved sharing with you.

And I love knowing that you and I can be assured that *God Is Able*.

At the very beginning of these pages, I asked you to *Tell Me* your personal *Its*. I told you some of mine, and I'm sure you didn't have much trouble naming yours.

Now, these few pages and hours later, we've grabbed those issues by the shoulders, spun them around, and made them face the full light of God's Word. And while they may still be present there in the room with you, they shouldn't look exactly the same way they did before.

Not after these two spectacular, powerful, life-transforming, faith-building verses in Ephesians 3.

Most likely your *Its* have had the habit of carving out their own independent space in your life, expecting to be treated differently, exempt from the promises of Scripture that apply to everything else. Like opposite poles of a magnet, they've juked and dodged around your faith, always seeming to be a step ahead of what God could actually do about them.

But "now" their free rein is over. The *TIME* has come to connect them with God's ability.

They've always expected your full attention. They've taken up the couch, the kitchen, the hallways, your storage space, your overnight hours—sometimes screaming, sometimes shaming, sometimes stomping in at the worst possible moments. (Your weakest moments.) And yet as difficult as they've been to deal with, you haven't felt as though you could afford to take your eyes off them—not for one second.

But they're no longer entitled to dominate the conversation. You've turned down their volume by *TURNING* "unto Him."

Your *It* problems have probably seemed to defy resolution. They've mocked your attempts at steady endurance, insisting they have the staying power to outlast whatever confidence you can muster up, even on your best days. They've pointed to their presence alone as ample proof, not only of God's lack of ability, but worse—His lack of concern.

And yet you've finally seen through their showboating now. The One "who is able" is the One who's telling you the *TRUTH*.

At times you may have decided you just need to live with *It*. Maybe you've felt like you deserve it—a punishment of some sort. Maybe you've just been taking it for so long, you don't know any different. You've concluded this is simply "the way life is." It's the best you can expect. You have your good days and your bad days, and that just needs to be good enough.

But it doesn't get to define your expectations anymore. Because there's a *TRANSCENDENCE* to God's ability. He can do things that are "exceeding abundantly beyond."

Maybe it hasn't been anything huge, just a lot of little things bunched together: nagging aches and pains, ongoing frustrations, sluggishness, an overall yet ambiguous sense of being stuck and rutted. But with people dying and divorcing and dealing with such serious dysfunction all around, you've been trying not to get in God's way or bother Him with your petty problems.

But you've changed your tune now about the small stuff. Because God cares about "all that we ask or think." You've opened up the *TOTALITY* of your life to His ability.

These problems, issues, and concerns have gotten so good at making you feel so powerless. They have drained your energy and overwhelmed your patience and reserves. They have stolen your sleep, steamrolled your self-worth, and sabotaged your sense of sanity. You had always been able to stand tall in faith no matter what happened . . . that is, until *It* came along.

But you've had it. It's held you down for the last time. You're ready to tap into the *TURBO* power of God. "The power that works within us" is at work in you too. You're turning these trials of life into a *TRIBUTE* offering to the Lord.

And "to Him be the glory."

"In the church and in Christ Jesus."

"To all generations forever and ever."

Yes, Lord.

But before I put the final "Amen" on this book, I want you to size up what these finishing touches actually mean for you. When we started out on this journey together, when we were talking about and comparing our *Its,* that was just a way of getting acquainted. Setting the table. But now that we're standing on the other side of Paul's massive, monumental declaration of God's wonder-working power, I want to propose a new resolution for you. And for me.

The next time somebody asks you how *It's* going, I want you to think about giving a new kind of answer. From now on, *It* will no longer refer to your biggest, hairiest problem. It won't stand for the longing or the lack that's become almost as much of an identifying mark on your life as the height and hair color details on your driver's license. It won't represent your sickness or your sorrow—the one that everybody seems to know about. Or that almost *nobody* knows about.

That's not *It* anymore.

It . . . is God's ability.

Whenever you talk about what's going on in your life, what if instead of your troubles and heartaches filling up all the subject lines, God's name and activity took center stage? What if you had a lot more to tell about His work than about your worries?

I'm not talking about becoming somebody who denies they've got any problems, just someone who chooses to deliberately, intentionally, *verbally* give God's power top billing in their conversation. We've been sufficiently reminded now—beyond a doubt—that "God is able," and so we ought to have a lot more to say about His ability and His love and His power and His sustaining mercy and strength than we ever should say about how bad we've got it.

I want to be talking about Him, not *It*.

Don't you?

He should be the new *It* that garners our attention and conversation.

- ❖ Celebrate the *freedom* His ability gives you and how it helps you stay content through whatever season of life you're experiencing.
- ❖ Give Him glory for the *boldness* and *fearlessness* He pumps through you, even when everything else inside is yelling for you to panic and run away.

❖ Talk up His *miracles* rather than just moving on to the next problem.

❖ Let people hear why your *confidence* in Him is so well placed, even when you're dealing with such difficult things.

❖ Relax in the hope infused into you by God's power, no matter what your today or tomorrow looks like.

If I'm going to be an open book about anything, I want it to be about how blessed I am that I am loved by, cared for, and sheltered under the mighty, sovereign grace of God.

The world we live in may not have a very high, personal view of His ability. They may not think He can operate supernaturally in people's lives anymore, But I know He can.

And so do you.

Our God is ABLE, I'm telling ya.

And.

That's.

All.

There.

Is.

To.

IT.

Navigate the Unexpected

Life Interrupted shows how to embrace the amazing freedom and fulfillment that comes from going with God, even when He's going against your grain.

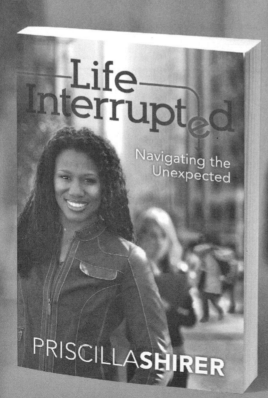

Life Interrupted

Navigating the Unexpected

PRISCILLA SHIRER

Every WORD matters™
BHPublishingGroup.com

from the pew
to the pavement

Priscilla Shirer

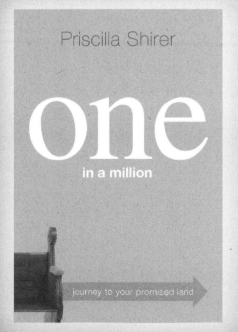

one

in a million

journey to your promised land

Will you be the one?

Popular bible teacher Priscilla
Shirer goes beyond talk to
show how we can apply what
we hear in church every week
to how we live every day.

Every WORD Matters™
BHPublishingGroup.com

NEW YORK TIMES
BESTSELLING BOOK

INSPIRED BY THE MOVIE
COURAGEOUS

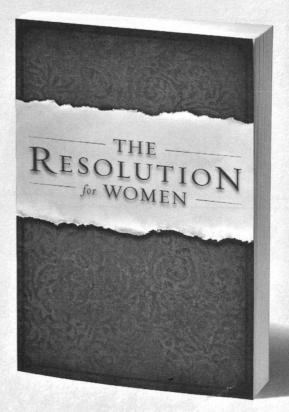

Popular author and speaker
PRISCILLA SHIRER
challenges all women to
thrive in God's beautiful,
eternal calling on their lives.

See How Other Women's
Lives Have Been Impacted
& Share Your Own Story

 ResolutionForWomen

© 2011 SHERWOOD PICTURES MINISTRY, INC. A MINISTRY OF SHERWOOD BAPTIST CHURCH, ALBANY, GEORGIA. ALL RIGHTS RESERVED.

Pastor
Murray

Kurt Gabrielson
        Dr. Prall
        South Denver Neurosurgery
            Sky Ridge
        Littleton Adventist
        720-638-7500
        _____

        PA: Susanna

        Joyce   Chaplain
            203-8583654

St John's - on French St - Sally